Dying to Live

Dying to Live

By

Moira Scott

ISBN 0 9531563 3 8

Copyright Moira Scott 1998
Words for 'By Your Side' N.&T. Richards
Copyright Thankyou Music 1989

Published by:

Information PLUS,
Finstown, Orkney. KW17 2LH

Printed by:

The Orcadian Limited, Hell's Half Acre,
Hatston, Kirkwall, Orkney. KW15 1DW

Acknowledgements

I'm ever grateful for life, having come through at the other end of a terminal disease healed, words cannot express my wonder and amazement at the many events that took place over that year to bring me to complete healing.

Thank you is not enough to say to all the people who helped, prayed, loved, cared, and brought words of comfort and life to me during the dark days when my life was almost gone. It is not possible for me to name you all but a special mention has to go to my lovely family. You were always there when I needed you, and your love and presence gave me a reason to go on and find life even in the face of death, you were and are my pride and joy in this life and I will forever treasure these memories in my heart, thanks. To Rob, Fiona, and Emma Dawson for their indescribable generosity and love accommodating me and my family over that time of great need, thanks. Mums and dads, sisters and brothers, nieces and nephews, doctors, nurses, friends, church, etc, etc. Thank you to everyone, the list is endless. I do not make any claim to be an inspirational author, this is merely my attempt to bring some hope to others facing similar trials.

In " *Dying To Live* ", it is my prayer that you the reader will find something to help you through the changing seasons of your lives too.

Moira Scott

PAST & PRESENT

I remember the beauty of hot, sunny days and running through fields of lush green grass with the warm wind blowing gently in my hair. I remember listening to the distant calling of the curlew and lapwing, being conscious of the freedom welling up inside me, as I sensed the same wonderful liberty of being one with everything around me. To this day, the incredible sense of the solitude and wonder of this experience still has the power to transport me instantly back to my childhood days when I played the hours away with my sisters in the fields of my father's farm.

I was the second child in a family of seven, six girls and one boy and my childhood was happy and secure. Having so many sisters meant there was never a need for other close friends and when we weren't helping on the farm, we spent endless hours at the seashore just below our house, inventing and playing all sorts of fun games.

 Life on our farm brought us very close to nature and the ever changing demands which the seasons placed on the rural lifestyle, helped me to be adaptable, which is a character trait that aided me to respond to the many changes that would mark my future life.

A large family is inclined to develop a great sense of responsibility for the younger members of the family and this it did in me, not unhealthily, but in a wholesome way which has contributed positively to my character and which is affirmed today in many aspects of my life. In retrospect, I can see how my early life's experiences had a much more powerful and far reaching purpose than I could ever have imagined.

As a family we attended church and Sunday school and I certainly believed in God and Jesus, but my childhood thoughts of God were that He was distant, a God who lived up in Heaven but who would be there when I needed Him. The one time this philosophy was challenged remains clearly in my mind. It was a time when a series of meetings, led by two ladies, were held in our local primary school. I went every night and so enjoyed the lively songs they taught us which were quite unlike anything we had in our church at that time. So powerful was the impact of the simple ministry of these two ladies in my life that I can still sing every word of those songs and quote the Bible verses I learned at that time. At the end of the week there was a special time for anyone who had felt God had been speaking to them, to stay behind for a prayer time. I was about eight or nine years old at the time and, that Friday, my friend and I had agreed together in the playground at school, to stay behind after the meeting to pray with the ladies. That night I knelt in the little primary school and repeated a prayer asking Jesus to come into my heart, and I believe He did.

Many folk view faith and belief in God as a very private thing, and maybe even more so here, in Orkney, where our culture causes us to be a shy and reserved people who are reluctant to speak openly about our feelings, whether they be spiritual or emotional. Our past has moulded us and we have adopted our own ways of coping with our spiritual, emotional and physical needs. In the pages of this book I want to break free from some of those long held silences in the hope that Orcadians reading this will see that underneath the exterior of our lives, whatever our background or nationality, we are all the same. We each have the same need to be accepted and loved, to belong and work, to find a meaning and purpose fulfilling our lives.

It is from this background that I have come, ever grateful for the good things it has produced in me and thankful for that night in the peedie (little) Rendall school when I asked Jesus into my life. At the time I had no idea of the eternal consequences which that one small act would play in the course my life was to take, and being in a family where we didn't speak much about deep spiritual things, I never felt I could talk about the episode without embarrassment, and so it was never mentioned. Nevertheless, something deeply significant had taken place within me, the truth of which I was not to know for many years.

I grew up, left school and came home to work on my father's farm. I had no sense of direction and therefore, this seemed the natural thing to do. While there were things I intensely disliked about farm work, I really enjoyed most aspects of it, and I expect it's like that in every job. My life drifted on with varying teenage interests such as youth club, badminton and young farmers, and many teenage fancies and dreams were accomplished through them all in some way.

At eighteen I felt, as many other eighteen year olds have felt, that

I was well and truly on the shelf since nobody suitable for me to marry had come on the scene and thus I should content myself to a life of single solitude. It is so sad that young girls can be so desperately misled as to think that everything life has to offer us is tied up in whether we have a husband or not. Perhaps this is not so much the norm these days, or maybe it's more subtly disguised. Whatever, there was a strong desire in me to meet the man of my dreams.

It is so strange that these desires within us are so strong. Well, perhaps it is not so strange, as finding a partner for life appears to be one of the most normal inner drives human beings have, one that is built into the very core of our being. Surely, this was created in us by God so that woman and man together, as husband and wife, could express the full nature of God and in becoming one flesh, declare to the world this mystery. If this is so, then it is no wonder that we long to find that one person compatible to us, to spend the rest of our lives here on earth with.

I can assure you I had no such sense at that time, but attraction in itself is a mystery, and I began to notice a certain young man. The very first time I saw him I felt a powerful attraction to him. I knew the sort of person I wanted and wasn't prepared to settle for less than the standards I had set in my heart. Now here he was, just the sort of person I'd been yearning for. How did I know? I don't know. The first time I saw Ivan was at the local young farmers club. I had never met him and yet I had such an attraction to him, but would he notice me?

That was my nineteenth summer and in the August the young farmers held their annual rally where the girls competed in various types of crafts and abilities and the boys exercised their skills in such things as tractor driving and feats of strength. Everyone joined in the stock judging, myself included. I had a keen eye for a good animal so I liked the challenge. So long as I was in a group and not singled out, I felt fairly confident. A shy person, I secretly found myself strongly attracted to a young man who appeared to be as shy as me, but with a certain quiet confidence, which I lacked.

Much to my amazement, I had won the stock judging the previous year, even though it was the first time I'd ever done it. This year, however, the young man won it. After the day's activities, a presentation and dance were held in a local hotel. These functions were always very exciting and good fun, and this one proved to be no exception. It was then that I really met Ivan and it seemed pretty obvious that he liked me, too. Even though we exchanged conversation for some time, no more came of it for a while.

One night, as I went to bed with thoughts of Ivan in my head, I uttered a simple request "God, if you're there, would it be possible for You to work out how I could get to meet Ivan again, and is he the right person for me?" I wasn't into prayer in a big way at that time, but I still had that childhood awareness of God being there for me when I needed him. It wasn't uppermost in my mind but occasionally from August to December I either met or bumped into Ivan by chance. In the new year, he came down to our home with some friends. Needless to say, I was delighted when, on his way out, he asked me if I would like to go to the pictures with him. There began a wonderful romance which from that day to this has not ceased to grow and mature into something far beyond my wildest dreams and aspirations. We were married the following August, and now, twenty eight years later, are as committed to each other as we were then.

Ivan was a farmer also, and worked on his father's farm. His was a family of seven boys and one girl. They were churchgoers, but much more serious about their faith than my family. They were Baptist folk and their Christianity was more a way of life which affected every area. At the time I thought it was a bit extreme, but I started to go along to their church and found I really liked it. The people were warm and friendly and I began to attend the women's meetings. I felt very included but somehow I knew I wasn't quite the same as them, although I didn't know why.

Soon we started a family with Lynn arriving first, followed two years later by Sharon. We were so happy with our two girls, as well as with each other and life, on the whole, was good. A couple of years after Sharon was born, a series of meetings were held in the Baptist church by well known evangelist, Ian Leitch. I wanted to go, but being on a farm servant's small wage we couldn't afford the cost of £5 each. In the end, Ivan's mum paid for us, making it possible for us to go. The meetings had the very American title of A NEW LIFE SEMINAR.

I went most nights and Ivan went when he could. Ian Leitch proved to be such an interesting person with a wonderful sense of humour, and we marvelled at the ordinary, yet inviting, way he explained the validity of the Bible and gave extraordinary proof of its truth. Slowly I began to discover the truth for myself. No one had ever explained the whole story to me from beginning to end in this way, and by the end of that week I knew God was speaking to me in a very personal way. On the last night of these meetings we were asked to fill in a simple form about our faith which asked such things like how long I had been a Christian etc. While filling out the form, I was reminded of that night in the Rendall school where I had asked Jesus into my heart and I became aware that God was stirring me again, but in a new way.

As I drove home that night I felt a deep excitement inside me. I went to pick Ivan and the girls up from my folk's house, and in the car we spoke of all that we heard at the meetings. We lay talking together in bed that night, attempting to reason in our hearts and heads the overwhelming feeling that we ought to follow God in a new and deeper way. For us it seemed like this was the only way forward, as though if we didn't give our lives completely to God now, we might not get another chance.

There in our bed, on January 25, 1976, Ivan prayed a prayer asking Jesus to touch us afresh and to let us know for certain that He had come into our lives. The reality of this experience was instantly confirmed as we were overcome with floods of tears while the Lord Jesus touched our hearts in the most loving and gentle way. We knew, beyond the faintest shadow of doubt, that as we were willing to surrender ourselves to God, He in turn came to us to fulfil the promise He made in John's gospel, chapter 14 v. 23 'and We (Father, Son, Holy Spirit) will come to you and make Our home in you.' This is an amazing truth, that God would send His Holy spirit to live in ordinary human beings like you and me. It is uniquely divine yet so simply true .

So it is from this background, that I would like to take you on a journey which speaks of a life changed from normal, every-day and hum-drum to a time of great challenge and triumph. In every life there are events and feelings which stretch people from the depths of despair to the great hope that, beyond all we see and know, there is a greater purpose and plan being worked out. It is with great excitement that I look back to see the intricately woven tapestry which was invisible to me at the time.

It is my earnest prayer that all who read this book will find new hope and comfort in the face of seeming impossible circumstances, knowing that our God is the God of impossible

A PROGRESSIVE PROGNOSIS

Our family home buzzed constantly, the days filled with people in and out. Coming from a big family it was almost second sense to be hospitable and I liked it that way. My mum and dad were very welcoming homely folk, my memories of my growing up years are filled with many happy days and nights spent in the company of friends and neighbours. It was in these times that I gained my love for people which remains with me today.

The summer of 1990 had been long and busy with lots of visitors and now, in October, we needed a holiday. How tired I seemed to be that summer. It was an unusual, heavy tiredness and whenever I got the chance I would fall asleep. I seemed unable to keep myself awake. I decided that this must be what it felt like to be 40, with four children and farm life, plus the demands of church life to consider plus the constant flow of visitors passing through our home. Feeling that a dose of iron would put me right, I went to the doctor. I explained my extreme tiredness as well as the constant terrible itching which had gradually worsened over the last few years. Dr Stuart took a blood test and sent it away expecting the results back in a week.

As I drove back from the surgery that night I thought again the very same thoughts I'd had when I was a child, remembering the sunny summer days running through the fields with the wind blowing my hair and the exhilaration of the sense of complete freedom. I was overwhelmed with the desire for wanting everything to stay exactly that way forever.

Two days later, while sitting with friends from our church, Mike and Helen Chisholm, the phone rang. It was Dr Stuart, and I was surprised to hear that she had the results back already. The tests had shown that I was very anaemic with other abnormalities. She suggested the possibility of hepatitis or a liver or gall bladder disease, definitely something obstructive. Shocked at the speed of the test results, we sat and discussed the various possibilities and all the while I just knew it had to be pretty serious to demand such an urgent call. I had gone to the doctor many times during the last few years because of this annoying itch, only to be told it was an allergy or nervous complaint. It had seemed to me that something was somehow under my skin or in my blood, and although I frequently felt that something was wrong inside, I never took it too seriously.

The following week I had an appointment with the surgeon who suspected an enlarged liver and advised a liver biopsy in Aberdeen. My own doctor thought it would be a liver disease called Primary Billiary Cirrhosis, she prescribed a dose of iron tablets and arranged my trip to Aberdeen Hospital.

We decided to make a family holiday out of it and stayed together at Ivan's sister's home in Kintore, near Aberdeen. Their family and ours had always been close and we always enjoyed time spent together over the years. As well as being family, Doreen and Gordon are also very special friends, and we have shared many joys and pains. Sharing the same faith has also deepened our times together. We had valued them and their support, but over the next months they were going to prove more special than ever before.

This was one of our most relaxing holidays ever and already I felt much better. We did fun things but my stamina was not good, especially when we went for a walk up Ben Achie. I was positively breathless after a few stiff climbs and sat down for frequent rests. I became very frustrated with myself, not realising this was a symptom of my disease. Walking along the street was very tiring and I would often end up crying because I felt so useless. Apart from these little things, we had a lovely break which was just what we were needing. It was a concentrated, relaxing, family time.

My appointment at Woodend Hospital for the biopsy and several other tests was to be the start of long, endless queues of people waiting for their turn for whatever test. The time dragged as I just sat around doing nothing but stare at the walls, looking at folk who were much more ill than I was. The way people speak has always interested me and I find it very easy to pick up the accent of the people wherever I go. I loved the Aberdonian accent and soon got the hang of it, with particular help from an old Aberdonian lady who was in the bed next to me. She made me laugh as she referred to the patients as inmates, especially as I had begun to wonder if I had arrived in prison rather than hospital. This lady used to say of the doctors that " if hid's nae yir blaaud they wir efter it wis yir stooauls". This seemed a reasonable statement to me at the time .

The biopsy was the last test, and entailed removing a very small slither of the liver by using a very long syringe inserted just below my ribs between the diaphragm and abdomen. It was a very skilled job, during which time I had to lie completely still and flat for twelve hours in order to prevent bleeding. I found lying still difficult and concluded that I really hated hospitals and the sooner I was out the better.

The hospital was full of the stories of ordinary people battling with their health. I talked a lot with a woman from Westray who had been down there for weeks with leukaemia. I was glad that I would not be staying for weeks. Across the ward from me was a very sad young girl in her teens with an eating disorder. She had refused to eat and looked awful so she had to be fed liquid through her nose. She had asked for her mother to stay away. I felt such sorrow for this young person, so overcome with this terrible disease that she had no will to live. This was my first encounter of this kind and little did I know that it would be the first of many.

My specialist, Dr Sinclair, was almost certain I had P.B.C., an incurable progressive liver disease, but was considering the necessity of one more test which involved putting a lens down my throat to check the veins carrying blood up through the oesophagus. I didn't really want to have it and so I was pretty relieved when they decided not to bother. That was the end of that for the time being and now I could get back to normal and wait for the final results. I seemed to have amazing peace, but couldn't make up my mind if it was really peace or just that the shock had not hit yet.

Coming home, I decided I wanted to keep life as normal as possible. I got stuck into a knitting machine course in Kirkwall which proved to be a great diversion for me and a completely new interest. My sister Rosalind started at the same time, so we went in together and it was good for taking my mind off myself as well as getting me out of the house. I picked it up very quickly and soon produced my first garment.

This new concept of being an ill person was very hard to get to grips with, since I was also reasonably fit and able to do all my work. The results of the tests said that I had a lot of years left in my liver so there was no immediate danger to my life, therefore I went on the assumption that it would be a long time before there would be any drastic signs of deterioration. However, little did I know what lay round the corner.

DYING TO LIVE

It was the end of November and I had spent the day at my knitting class. I had been feeling miserable all day and suspected that I had a stomach bug. On the way home I had a heavy nose bleed, something which had become commonplace over the last year, so I thought nothing of it. Arriving home, I was feeling a bit dizzy and faint and went to have a lie down as I didn't feel like having any tea. After an hour or so, I got up again and came downstairs to lie on the sofa, still feeling pretty miserable although a little better. It was evening now and Ivan had gone off to a church house group meeting.

About ten o'clock I was concerned when I noticed a little blood in some spit I brought up, and then a little more. My 13 year old son, Jonathan and my daughter, Sharon, who was 16 at the time, were still up but James, the youngest, now 10, had gone to bed. I knew something was wrong so Sharon quickly got me a basin as I felt very sick, while I phoned the doctor and Ivan at house group. He arrived just before the doctor. In this way, the most unusual, challenging and uncertain time in my entire life began.

Here I was to understand in a new way what it meant that in dying I found life, strange as this may sound to you, yet the truth that even in death we find life and life in abundance.

Just after the doctor arrived I was very, very sick, mostly blood. The doctor was trying frantically to get a drip fixed up but my veins had collapsed and gone flat due to the heavy bleeding, so he wasn't managing very well. Realising by now that this was very serious, I asked Ivan to pray for me. As we prayed, I lay there feeling my life's blood draining out of me. It was the strangest feeling but not scary, just peaceful inside in a way that is difficult to explain. I prayed about anything that might be working against God to take my life, but also that if it was God's will that I die and go home to be with Him, I was ready to go. This happened so quickly and I prayed in tongues, which is a language God has given to Christians to speak when we run out of our own words to pray. It's a gift of the Holy Spirit that is referred to in 1 Corinthians 14 v 1 to end of the chapter.

As I prayed in this way, I noticed how quickly the doctor got the needle into my vein although he was still looking pretty grim. It was probably a good thing I couldn't see myself. My blood pressure had dropped drastically and I had come out in a cold sweat. I felt I was dying and I knew only God could keep life in me. Suddenly, I began to feel a little better and I just knew Jesus was there. The doctor had a look of surprise as my blood pressure stabilised. Jesus had touched me, He was in this, He cared for me and He answered my prayer. The immediate emergency was over, but what a shock.

During all this fuss Ivan was laying his hand on my head, praying. I can only imagine what was going through his head in this crisis and the poor children having to witness such trauma. I was quite unaware of all that was happening to them because I was so caught up in myself.

Once I stabilised, the doctor sent for an ambulance and I was carried off in a stretcher and transported to the local hospital where another drip was fixed up, plus some blood matching for a transfusion. I had to go to Aberdeen where they had all the equipment necessary for my treatment. Even though I was feeling alive, I was definitely shaken because I had no idea this would be likely to happen, or that it was a common symptom of my disease. I wish I had been prepared for it, but it was like a bolt out of the blue and I wondered how I would have reacted had I known in advance. Perhaps on hindsight it was better that I didn't know because the stress of knowing would have been very hard to cope with at the early stages, since it was hard enough coming to terms with an incurable illness.

Through it all I was very alert, not realising how close to death I had been. I was fairly resigned to the fact that Aberdeen was the place to be, so as the little Loganair plane raced along the runway I prayed again for the Lord to be with me. I would have preferred Ivan to be there but it had all happened so suddenly and he needed to stay with the family and break the horrible news to James in the morning.

What a shock it must have been for them. Anyhow he couldn't

be with me so accompanying me on the flight were two nurses and a doctor, plus a bag of blood swinging from a hook. One of the nurses, a young student named Mary, was so special to me. There was something about her that I warmed to instantly, her loving special touch was exactly what I needed at the time. She felt like family, just like I would expect a daughter to be, just like Lynn, our eldest, and I wondered if I would ever see her again.

The flight took about 45 minutes and we arrived in Aberdeen at 2.am. We were met at the hospital by Dr. Kennedy, a young student doctor who was special in every way. It is routine for the nurse taking a patient's details to ask for religion and church and when I said I was a Christian who attended a Fellowship church, she mentioned to me that her mother went to a Pentecostal church although she didn't herself. I touched her arm with my hand and she and I both knew that God had spoken to her through this brief encounter.

There was to be little peace that night as the nurses maintained a vigilant check on drips, blood pressure etc. The next day I went for treatment to seal off the veins which had burst in my oesophagus. Apparently these varicose veins were caused by pressure building up in the veins because the main vein bringing the flow of blood up through the oesophagus was obstructed by the disease PBC. It was these veins which had burst, causing the bleeding which I didn't realise could have been fatal. The veins were to be sealed off using an endoscopy, injecting some stuff into these burst veins to stop any further bleeding. This was horrible, I will never forget the taste of the anaesthetic spray squirted into my throat to deaden it for the endoscope to go down more easily. I feel sick yet when I think of it.

This was the first of many of these treatment sessions and as I went under the drug I prayed that God would come with me into my subconscious and protect me. On this ward there was a young lady, Dr. Sewell. One day, as she reached over me, I noticed a little dove badge on her lapel. Realising she was a Christian, I ventured to ask her about it. She talked a bit about herself and told me the doctor in charge of the ward, Dr. Murchison, was a Christian too. She assured me I was in good hands and I felt very blessed, knowing God's hand in so many ways already. By now I had a mass of blood drips and fluid drips in both arms, and I was beginning to feel like a pin cushion. The miracle that I was still alive was becoming more evident.

As the news got round at home about my emergency, so the cards and letters began to flow into the ward, along with cards for my 41st birthday which was in a few days time. The amount of cards was unbelievable, everyone on the ward thought I must have lots of friends. I was reminded again what a blessing it is to belong to a loving family and church at times like these and I still have all the cards as a reminder of that time.

Our eldest daughter Lynn, now 19, was at Northern College in Aberdeen doing her B. Ed. in primary teaching and she became my constant support and strength at this time. I'm aware of how hard it must have been for her to fit in her many visits, plus all her study, but without her my life would have been very lonely and cut off from home. She was then, and is still now, a delight and a valuable treasure.

Having farmed the children out to my sisters' homes, Ivan arrived at the hospital on my birthday with a special surprise. Anyone who knows Ivan is aware that he isn't very into surprises, so this was touching for me. It was a small parcel and inside was the most lovely eternity ring, gold with six beautiful sapphires. It was a perfect fit. He knew the size of my wedding ring finger was the same as his little finger. I wore it all the time after that as a constant reminder of his love for me and many people commented on how beautiful it was. It was just the sort of ring I would have chosen for myself. Ivan stayed a week, hoping that I would be able to go home with him, but I needed more treatment. This was the first of many built up hopes that ended in disappointment for us all.

Over the next three weeks I had treatment three times, and always felt very groggy after the drug dose which meant I could eat nothing for hours after, but they assured me they were getting on top of the problem. Helen and mum came down the day of my third dose and it was so good to have them there. They just sat beside my bed all day and every now and then I opened my eyes and smiled. I found it so healing to have family around.

Progress was good and on the 15th December I was allowed home with them just in time for Christmas. It was oh, so good, to be home again and see that the bairns had put the tree up along with all the decorations, etc. Howe looked good to me and felt better than ever before. Home cheers the heart like nowhere else. One Friday evening the kids went over to my sister Helen's and I lay down on the same sofa I had nearly died on three weeks before, in my head still trying to come to terms with the sudden changes that had taken place, now relaxing in Ivan's company until the family came home, what a precious memory, home has such a way of healing the heart, bringing hope and security.

There is something about hospital life that robs us of the comfy, private place we find in our homes and I have often wondered through my own experience, how this aspect of illness could be improved, since for me it was such a crucial part of the healing process. Hospitals are wonderful places when we need them, but hospital beds, such slim hard things with plastic and cotton sheets, are starched and cold. My own bed was sheer luxury compared to that. Tension and anxiety breed in hospital because it is so out of the normal routine, and being a reserved sort of person, I found it increasingly difficult to relax.

I had become very weak, the oesophagus had taken a battering and the shock of the whole experience, coupled with the fear of the like happening again, had made me tense and nervous. I became even more sleepy, too, so I spent a lot of time dozing. I didn't know if it was caused by the drugs or just the way my life was going to be from now on. The bliss of being home only lasted about a week before I began to bleed again. Once again, I was off on another emergency flight, leaving Lynn and all the rest upset. What was God doing? I didn't know. I had so been upset. What was God doing? I didn't know. I had so been looking forward to being home for the festive season and seeing all the presents under the tree!

This must have been a sad and lonely time for the kids but I had no choice, I wanted to be home, yet, I had to go. What a mess, such a tearing at my heart was going on. I was given another dose of treatment and Ivan came down to spend Christmas with me. What a blessing and support he was to me. With his quiet personality, I suppose he will never really know the depth of strength of character he has and how much I drew comfort from his presence.

Christmas on the ward was different. We had all the trimmings, plus Dr. Kennedy as Santa with presents for everybody. The staff made such an effort for us and in the evening people came round to sing carols, but there was such an aching in my heart for my family and home. Nevertheless, I was home for hogmanay and New Year. We had Christmas dinner on New Year's day and I had a delicious piece of salmon, which the family did all by themselves.

My Mum and Dad came over to stay at Howe and it was good for all the kids to be together at home as well as doing mum and dad good. Whatever age your family are, they are still your little children and that's what I was to them. It was so easy for them to feel useless at times like these, and their being able to help was very important. Dad, who is an expert shepherd, looked after the sheep for Ivan. It was second nature to him and I should say it wasn't the big flock, just the pure bred Suffolk flock which was a small number in comparison but they needed looked after and dad held the fort. Parents always play a special role in our lives to bring that stability and constant caring. A mum is always a mum no matter what age we are and at this time in my life I was ever grateful for my parents. They were a constant source of love and support to us all over that time and rose to every new challenge with commitment and willingness, far beyond the call of duty, a labour of love, from the heart.

Now I was home again I wondered how long it would last, as this was the first time I had made it for the full three weeks before the next treatment. It was such an achievement to go the full time without bleeding. Lynn was back in Aberdeen, but I didn't have a long stay and was soon back home again. I was experiencing a lot of tension as the sudden bleeds were becoming all too common place. The bleeding would start and I would be off on another emergency flight again and again it seemed. In the past it had always been ward 27 but this time I was taken to ward 13. Dr. Sewell had informed me she was to be moved and I might not see her again. This made me very sad, because in unfamiliar places we look for something familiar, and I had grown to love and trust this lovely Christian doctor. Many times she would come back after ward rounds and chat to me. She treated me like a person and not an experiment and I really liked her. In a strange environment, just knowing she was there gave me confidence.

I absolutely hated the way the nurses moved the beds around on operating or admission days, especially when I had just begun to feel comfy in my own little space. I made my bed area my own territory, and just felt comfy when I was moved. I don't suppose the staff knew what it made me feel like, but being already out of sorts, this practice made it all so much harder to bear for me because nothing was normal. Dr. Sewell and I exchanged addresses but I wondered if I would ever see her and Dr. Kennedy again.

Ward 13 was alien to me and I disliked it instantly. I don't know why, perhaps the strangeness of the unfamiliar surroundings, but I felt uncomfortable. Possibly all the tripping about was beginning to get me down. Until now I had been coping well in most ways, but in this ward I just couldn't stop crying and I felt so alone. I felt desperate for someone from home to be there for me. I'd never experienced this weird feeling before. When I phoned home, I cried and it upset Ivan. When Lynn came in I cried and it upset her. When I cried it upset me. I felt ward 13 was a God forsaken hole of a place, but really, I never bothered to look for Him there. Fear, fear, fear! I had become so fearful. Even though I had been dealing with all sorts of fears through my life, and especially these last months, here was another.

The doctor on this ward was a tall, dark, handsome, young man, but his bedside manner was coarse and abrupt and he certainly lacked grace. He made me feel very uneasy and a nuisance, which was just what I didn't need. Dr. Kennedy popped into the ward, what a nice surprise, someone familiar, sitting down on my bed he chatted away to me so friendly and normally. What a blessing he was and his appearance was so reassuring. He had been moved to this ward and told me there was another woman from Orkney in the ward with a chronic liver disease. When she was pointed out to me I was struck with fear. She looked awful and I was afraid to see myself in her. Her disease had made her unable to walk properly and her skin was all out in sores. I was unable to speak to her, terrified that this was how I was going to look in the future.

I found the strength to pray a simple prayer from 1 Corinthians 12 where it says, *'Offer your bodies as a living sacrifice.'* Lord, I give you my body. Once I had prayed, my heart changed and I began to think about what I was afraid of. After all, did it really matter what I looked like. I felt the voice of Jesus say to me, "I will love you always, no matter how you look. Offer yourself to Me and I will take care of how you look. Your body is mine and I will help you." Suddenly I knew the Lord's great love for this other woman and somehow her appearance didn't matter to me any more. I decided that the next time she went past my bed, I would talk to her. The Lord had completely changed my attitude. We talked and shared together and she told me she was hoping for a transplant so I promised to remember to pray for her. I heard some time later she never made it for a transplant.

There was an older woman in the bed next to me, who had seen me reading my Bible. She asked me what church I went to, and I thought she would never know what a Fellowship Church was.

So that I didn't have to go into a long explanation I said, "a sort of Baptist type church" and she replied that she went to the Bridge of Don Baptist. During our chat she told me her son went to The Deeside Christian Fellowship. 'God forsaken' had been my opinion of this ward, but now I knew He is always there if we will look for Him. It was during this visit that I began to realise that I was going through a time of grieving for my health. I would look at everyone who came in and out of the ward and remember what l it felt like to be well. Now I understood that this was what all the crying was about. It was necessary, although a very painful experience and it was the only time I experienced such deep agony of soul.

I was down in hospital for a week that time and only home for three days when the bleeding started again. Added to that, the extensive treatments meant I had to have some chemical mixture injected into the veins resulting in ulcers in my oesophagus causing increased bleeding. It became difficult to define whether the blood was coming from the veins or the ulcers. These ulcers took a few weeks to heal and added to the problem I was having swallowing my food, but at least the ulcers didn't require a trip to Aberdeen and this time I was admitted to the Balfour Hospital in Kirkwall, which was a pleasant change as I hadn't been there since my first bleed.

One interesting aspect of this visit was that I met Mary again, the student nurse who had been with me on the first flight. As she emptied out the contents of my bag she asked if I wanted my Bible out. My Bible always travelled with me, and this started off a conversation about my faith and the church I went to. I was amazed at how warm and understanding she was, and as we talked, she shared about her dad's ministry. It became apparent to me that this girl knew the truth of the gospel. What a joy it was to speak to her.

I was so glad to see her again and I felt inside that our meeting was more than coincidence. She definitely believed the same as me but didn't feel she could live it just now. She spoke of many answers to prayer, of miracles and healings. I was sure she would give all her heart to Jesus one day and decided I would pray for her when I remembered. We spoke of her love for nursing and the fact that she was awaiting her results of her last year's exams.

She was such a good nurse I was sure she would pass. The day I was going home the results came. I didn't see Mary to ask her how she got on, but another nurse told me everyone had passed except Mary. I saw her in floods of tears but had no opportunity to talk to her. I felt overwhelmed with compassion for this young girl, maybe because I have girls of my own. I could feel her disappointment and felt I would write to encourage her.

It had been lovely to have my friends and family on the spot to visit me during this spell in hospital. Rosie, a close friend whom I knew through our church, was in visiting me one day when I mentioned my desire for a book to write down all the 'peedie thowts' that were going through my mind, as well as the many lessons I had been learning which were deep and life changing.

The next day a nurse brought me a present and inside was a beautiful red notebook from Rosie. It was inscribed FOR MOIRA'S PEEDIE THOWTS, and this was the beginning of what you now see. Inside, on the first page, she had written 'Deuteronomy 8: Write it down Moira lest you forget'. It was good advice, although at the time I just didn't feel able to concentrate, so I was not very diligent, but it was the birthing of an idea and the reality of what you now see.

I was becoming very weary, feeling I needed a change, and so, for the first time in years I went to stay at my mum's for the weekend. It was really special and the downstairs bedroom looked so comfortable, warm and inviting. I felt very spoiled, being waited on hand and foot. It was just the break I needed, mum loved it and so did I.

I was now unable to do anything. I had been prescribed blood pressure tablets to relieve the pressure of the blood flow coming up through the oesophagus. These made me very lethargic most of the time. I had no energy and put it down to being ill, so when the doctors decided to take me off the tablets as they were doing me more harm than good, I felt so much better it was unbelievable. However, the reality was that I was very ill, and because of the slow progression of the disease over the years, I hadn't realised how ill I had been becoming.

Everything had to change and my interests were diverted to simple, low energy things. I had been a very active person and at home I had always done the caring for others. I had never been in the place where I had received much help or caring from others to any great degree. Now I found myself in great need of every kind, unable to be a wife, mother, sister, daughter, housewife or serving Christian. Everything that made me what I was, was no longer there. It had all suddenly been swept from under my feet and nothing was familiar. Everything about me was constantly changing, always uncertain, and I had become totally dependent on other people. I had no choice, this was life for me now.

Deep down inside me, however, there was always the knowledge that my life was God's and that He was the giver and sustainer of life. All of us, not just me, are in constant need of Him to give us our life. On our own we are completely unable to keep ourselves alive one more second, let alone another day.

I was seeing this more and more, understanding how fragile life is and that our time here on earth is not to map out as we choose. Although we may think we control our lives, we really have no hold on our life, but God does. We may even think we know this, as I thought I did, but my illness had caught me out fair and square. Until now, I had been in charge, and I hadn't truly grasped the truth until it became a personal experience, as you will understand if you've been in that situation.

Sometimes during spells in hospital I would feel inspired to write poems and here in Ward 13 I wrote the following poem which I called Life's Changes.

LIFE'S CHANGES

As I lie here and try to work out
What all this life change for me is about
And try as I will I cannot see
More than this day You've given to me

When I start to rush on and work out
What all this life change is about
I know that You're teaching to me
A secret I could not otherwise see

As I lie here, I think to myself
What it was like to be full of health
How different my thoughts they would be
And this lesson would not reach to me

I know I cannot change a thing
But my God can change anything
If He chooses to, my place is to do
The very thing He asks me to

To trust as I lie here and wait
And be content in whatever state
To rejoice in my heart and soul
And my body I leave to Your will

For you're making a better new me
As I lie here, this I can see

THE KIDS!

How my family had the strength to cope over these times never ceased to amaze me.

Lynn, our eldest daughter, was now in her second year training to be a primary teacher. She had always been a blessing to us, so it wasn't surprising that she was even more so during my illness. It is difficult enough for families to be away from home in normal circumstances without all the trauma of a critically ill mother. Lynn was very much a motherly influence over the others as she readily took on the burden of family responsibilities. She often spoke of the possibility of giving up her course to help the younger ones and we talked during her many visits to hospital about the reality of my dying, but never once did she allow me to harbour these thoughts. She was always so positive that I would recover. I liked her attitude but somewhere inside me I wondered if this was some form of denial of the fact that I faced the possibility of death at any time. However real the danger my life was in, it was reassuring to have positive people around me and Lynn was a special provision for me in Aberdeen. Her visits were such a joy, something to look forward to and an extra bonus to have my own child on the spot to chat to and laugh with, to share the good days and the bad. Just to see her beautiful smiling face warmed my heart and how I thanked God for this wonderful daughter.

She had been a very fearful child in the early years of her life and we had not been mature enough to deal with these fears. We had tried everything but had never really found the answer. She was six years old when we became Christians, and since having Jesus had made such a difference in every area of our lives, we suggested to Lynn that having Jesus in her life might be the answer to all her bad dreams and disturbed sleep. She prayed herself, asking the Holy Spirit to come and live in her and help her with her scary dreams. After that, whenever she was bothered with dreams, we would pray and ask the Lord to come and take them away and it worked. Such childlike faith is a lesson many adults could pay heed to, and in this way Lynn's young faith grew. It was not surprising then that now, during my time of illness, her faith became such a source of strength and comfort to me. Her own faith was shared with me as she prayed and kept me going over that time and I found her very presence brightened any day.

Our second daughter, Sharon, was in her fifth year at Stromness Academy doing her higher grades. She was left at home so often and seemed so able and grown up for only seventeen. I guess she was stretched to the limit emotionally and physically many times, but it was typical of her nature to conceal those deep feelings. I never feared for her as it seemed as if God had prepared her for this unusual and difficult time. She adjusted so well and became so capable, appearing to sail through the exam stresses even though she had the added pressure of the housework, and Ivan never had to wash a shirt or cook a meal. Under normal circumstances, many young people cannot cope with the pressures of life, and yet it was evident that my young family were adapting to the rigorous demands very well. I don't doubt that having a real and living faith is of utmost value and my children knew that, overall, God was there giving added strength in every situation.

Sharon had her own quiet faith. She, too, had asked Jesus into her life as a very young girl through Lynn's influence, and had never gone back on her decision. The Lord accepts the prayer of a little child and keeps them in a growing faith all through their lives. Sharon was always very sensitive to my feelings, even to the neglect of her own. It must have been so hard for her to pack my bag for all the emergency flights but she had it worked down to a fine art in the end. There was such a depth of pain in that young heart and many times she choked back the tears as we parted. Her letters and words of encouragement were so timely and I could always picture in my mind the things she would write about. I believed that God would surely bless her abundantly for all her love and care.

Jonathan, our eldest son, was now fourteen and in his third year at the Academy. With a nature that was so like his dad, but a lot more liberated, he always had us laughing as he joked in his light hearted manner, yet he was such a private person about his feelings. The times I spent at home over those weeks of illness gave me the opportunity to get a lot closer to him. His cooking ability was amazing for a boy and he preferred to be in the house rather than work out on the farm. This was a real provision for Sharon, otherwise her job would have been much harder.

It was great to see how they all pulled together in this way, and I don't know how Ivan would have coped without them. He had never been a man who could do many things inside the house because as a boy he was expected to work out on the farm. He'd been taught that was men's work. Jonathan's interest in domestic things slightly amused him but I thought it was wonderful. Typical of family life, it's likely they fought for the position of boss, but Ivan said they were great and they certainly looked after him well.

Jonathan and I had always had a good friendship because, although he had been a demanding small child, he had developed into a well adjusted youth. He had an incredible interest in electrical things as a child and as he grew older, his creativity had taken many different roads. He took up piano lessons and quickly had a natural ability so we often enjoyed his sudden bursts at the piano. It was his way of relieving tension and we grew to understand that the more the tension, the more vigorous the tune.

It was Sharon and Jonathan who witnessed my first traumatic bleed, an event which neither have spoken much about, although I have asked them from time to time with little success. Jonathan once wrote an essay for English about an unusual event in his life and he chose to write about that first night I took ill. The title was "That Night On The Sofa." It helped me so much to see it from his perspective as, until then, I had no idea of how deeply it was imprinted in his mind. He had written down some of the feelings of anger at God and also some of the distress of his own need for me, his mum, to be there for him. How normal, and yet how blind I had been to the needs of these lovely young children because I was so caught up in my own needs.

Our youngest child, James, was nine and the opposite of Jonathan in almost every way. He was his dad's pal and they did everything together. James loved to be out on the farm with his dad and didn't mind getting in a mess. He liked going fishing, playing football, and anything outdoors he was into. I felt for him the most I think, mainly because he was the youngest, or maybe it was just different. I'm sure he missed me but it was never very apparent, and it seemed that for him to be so engrossed in Ivan's work meant that I was never so close to him as I was to Jonathan. It was a strange contrast, but nice. We can never compare the boys or draw parallels because they are uniquely themselves, men born with their own destiny. They both had their own young faith in God, having made a childhood commitment, but it was obvious that their beliefs were shaken by all that was happening .

My sister, Helen, lived just a few miles away from us and our two families were about the same ages. Helen's boys and ours were constantly together, cousins are often closer than any other friend, indeed, almost like sisters and brothers. James was never lonely and Helen's became a second home for my kids. What a special gift sisters are and I have been blessed with more than most. I will never in this life be able to thank her for all the help she was over that time. By now she was coming in every other day to wash floors, mucky toilets etc. Unless you've lived on a farm, you will not appreciate the mess that gathers from day to day. Through our back door there is a constant trail of mud, straw, grass, silage and dung being dragged in on the rubber boots, and that is just one area of the house. As well as that, there is the dust caused by a solid fuel fire and the general untidiness made by a young family. Helen was a faithful friend and sister to me who seemed to find it a blessing to give to me in this way. I'm sure everyone of these acts of kindness and service done for me is recorded in heaven. Matthew 25:40 *'Assuredly I say to you, inasmuch as you did it to one of the least of these my children, you did it to me, says the Lord.'*

The Lord has given me such a great family that sometimes it moves me to tears even yet when I consider the sacrifices they all made for me during this time. This provision gave me strength to keep going over the most desperate times. They were a comfort and encouragement, they made me laugh and helped keep me alive by their presence, prayers and practical helps. Praise be to God for families, and especially mine.

SPRING

Spring was now approaching and we had been invited to Ivan's niece's wedding in February. My stay at mum and dad's had been very relaxing and timely, giving me renewed confidence to try different things again. We decided we would all go to Rosemary and Ronnie's wedding, so new outfits were bought for everyone. The wedding ceremony was to be in Dundee on March the 2nd. I was feeling the best I had since the first big bleed and ready to have some fun again. We would stay with Ivan's sister and her husband, Gordon and Doreen.

Over the last months of illness, their home had become a place of retreat for me, a welcome change from the alien hospital environment. They were a warm and loving couple so their home and family were a wonderful substitute for all that I had been missing of home. Many times they went out of their way to love me, driving me to and from hospital, liquidising my food, bringing me little presents, looking after Ivan on his many trips south. How true the saying "a friend in need is a friend indeed".

The Abbey Fellowship (as it was known then) in Aberdeen was their church, in which Gordon was a leader/elder. They had just planted a new church at that time in Dyce and this little church became a real lifeline to me. The people were so warm and friendly, taking me to their hearts in praying and caring for me. Their housegroup in particular, made me feel secure and I got to know some of them quite well by name over these frequent visits to Aberdeen. Gordon and Jean Skinner and Douglas and Fiona McIntyre often prayed encouragement into my life and provided a necessary supply of worship and fellowship for me.

This was another aspect of life I missed terribly, my home church. My close friends, the people I built my life around, were no longer there. Experiencing this served to show me how much I had depended on these people to prop me up. Although it's very important to have a church in which to grow and share close friendships, to develop and mature, I saw for the first time really, really clearly, that I needed to know that this faith I had was a personal, real, alive thing working in my life. I needed to understand that my faith was not primarily based on other people and their friendship but that it was mine, for me, and that's what mattered most right now. The question of my heart was whether it was enough to be just me and God. Did I know this? Did I believe this? Could I survive without this, up to now, essential ingredient of other people ?

A testing trial it was, but a necessary challenge which has changed this area in my life, dramatically. I found at every turn that Jesus proved to be more than any friend or church or family or any other prop I had hitherto used to give my life identity and meaning. Only time would tell if this was the reason for all my uncertainty.

THE WEDDING

At last the trauma and shock of the last few months was beginning to fade and heal, I was feeling the best I had done since the first haemorrhage. Gradually I was regaining strength but still not even half the energy I had known before and always the huge threat hanging over me of another big bleed.

We all set off to Dundee by car from Aberdeen to a wedding which was really lovely and everything went according to plan. The ceremony was Christian and Rosemary looked so beautiful, as did her sister Jean. We had some family photos taken at the church and later we went to a picturesque country hotel. I enjoyed the whole affair so much, the trip was such a welcome diversion from the normal preoccupation with myself, and it was so nice to see all of the Scotts.

Prior to the wedding I had been to Aberdeen for another check on my veins. Dr. Sinclair, who attended to me in the endoscopy unit, was very disappointed to tell me that the varices were enlarged again and I would need to come back much sooner than planned for my next treatment. So far I had never managed to go the full time set between each treatment without some surprise happening, but since I was feeling so well it didn't bother me too much, although I was disappointed.

I always hated the treatment, the taste of the anaesthetic which was sprayed in the back of my throat was awful. The back of my hand which had the drug drip attached to it was beginning to show signs of wear and tear. The veins in my arms and hands were not very good either, and sometimes the staff made a few attempts before they succeeded. Constantly over these months I had a sign hanging at the top of my bed "NIL BY MOUTH" because I wasn't allowed to eat before an endoscopy, or for four hours after. Understandably, I had lost a lot of weight, but thankfully I had been slightly overweight before this all happened so it wasn't as serious as it could have been if I'd been skinny already.

Even in all the difficulties and trials, I managed to keep a pretty positive attitude, always continually grateful for the wonder of modern medicine and all the varied treatments they used to make the illness more acceptable and pain free. All the blood drips and the saline drips which didn't exist not so long ago, were a lifesaver to me for which I thank the Lord .

Arriving home after the wedding and following the bad report from Aberdeen, I settled in to things at home. Now, with more strength, I felt able to do some light housework. The next trip south was to be in three weeks time and I desperately desired to make the full time. One morning, ten days later, I awoke with a terrible nausea and realised I had had another internal bleed during the night. I phoned the doctor who came instantly and took my blood pressure only to confirm that I had suffered a considerable blood loss and would need to go to Aberdeen on another emergency flight.

These flights were common place now and my original fear of flying had vanished completely, just being thankful for this immediate form of transport. It's a strange feeling up there beyond the clouds, somehow giving me an acute awareness of the Lord and his greatness. Added to the sense of the immense vastness of space and time, was the overwhelming security of knowing that this God was vitally interested in me. I became aware of His closeness and indwelling presence here with me on these many flights, ever close, ever near, His loving, unseen arms wrapped gently around me, and a sense of awe filled my being.

This was becoming all too familiar now, and Sharon could pack a case in record time. How hard these partings must have been for her, only a young teenager. She was so special to me, so brave and yet, in her eyes, I could see the hurt and uncertainty of an invalid mother getting to her. I suppose the fear of never seeing their mother alive again increased the strain of coping from day to day. Mums are such essential people in our youth. I vividly recall the rare occasions my mother wasn't at home when we arrived from school and the strange, lonely feeling it created deep within me. My family were no different, they were getting pretty sick of it all as well.

My illness was showing me more and more that my life could be snuffed out any day, any time, so the stress and uncertainty was showing on us all.

We simply had to live a day at a time. I was beginning to get the hang of this lesson at last. Constantly being reminded of the fact that my life was not my own but belonged to God, made me understand that I had to trust him. I didn't always like it, I didn't always want to, but I simply had no choice. Few of us are able to accept that we have no say in our future, we all like to make our plans and control events in our lives. I liked to look after my family and make the decisions for them, after all I was the best at doing that, they needed me and I needed them. Did God know what He was playing at? This was a very real question for me and I had to search for real answers. I knew some of the answers in my head, but now I needed to know if they were a living reality in my heart, because it's all very well to have all the answers but they count for nothing if they're not lived out in our own lives in a practical, everyday way.

Long ago, at the start of my Christian life, I came across a lovely piece of scripture, Psalm 139. The whole psalm became a wonderful revelation to me of God's plan and purpose for my life. Understanding it caused my life to take on a whole new meaning as I realised that God actually saw my life before I was born, that He knows everything about me. I found it amazing that He knows everything I'm going to say before I say it, that He knows all the days He has planned for me and that there is nowhere in all of creation that I can go to be out of His presence. It seemed reasonable to me, therefore, through all the ups and downs and twists and turns my life was taking, that nothing, absolutely nothing concerning me, was hidden from God or out of His ultimate control, and if that applied to me, then it did for all my family too.

This was a real lesson for me in putting into practice what I believed. My faith was stretching from being a head knowledge to a living, worked out reality. We never know how much hold we have over our own lives until we are at the point of losing it and then it's so clear to see just who is in charge and I knew now that it was certainly not me. Every breath we take is a gift from God, never to be taken for granted. I was realising more and more that my Father in heaven was looking after me and was interested in every detail of my life. This intimate care was revealed to me one day at the very onset of my illness, when I realised that if even the very hairs of my head are all numbered, why worry about the state of my liver. He made all my inward parts so this disease was no surprise to Him. TRUST, TRUST! CAN I TRUST THIS GOD WITH MY LIFE? Well, there was no other choice and I was in no place to come up with a better one. My choice was to TRUST and take each day as it came.

Now I was in Aberdeen again with more tedious blood tests and more sitting about waiting for my turn. I used to joke about them sucking so much out of me when there was so little in, but that's hospital routine. When tested, there proved to be a significant blood loss. This was not good news, although it was expected. I felt so alone that day, wondering when and where this was all going to end.

Away from home again, not allowed to eat and feeling so pathetic. The day dragged on and on so slowly, but now it was bedtime again and all of a sudden that same old feeling swept over me like that first night on the sofa in November. The extent of the sickness caused me to feel as if all my life was draining out of me and I began to vomit blood.

Suddenly buzzers went off and doctors and nurses came running, fussing around me, fixing up drips, etc. and asking if I wanted to phone home. I felt they sensed I was going to die and I certainly did feel like it. The mobile phone came rattling down the ward to my bedside and I tried our home number but there was no reply. I desperately wanted to talk to Ivan, I wanted tell him that I might not last through the night and to say goodbye. A mixture of feelings welled up in me. I knew that to die at this point in time would be the easy option, especially since, being a Christian, I knew that meant eternity in Heaven. I longed to be away from all this hassle, and to know the presence of the Lord forever was for me a very real and attractive future. With no response from home I rang dad, telling him I didn't think I was going to make it this time, and I knew he didn't want to believe me. I asked him to tell Ivan how poorly I was and lay back on the bed. Dad told me later that after I had called he got down on his knees and prayed to God that I would not die.

Now the same prayer came to my mind that I had prayed on that first night. "Father God, I feel like I'm dying, so I'm ready to come to be with you forever, but I know that only You are able to breathe life into me and I ask only that you will do as you please with me, whether to live or die." I remember very little after that, except being told that Dr. Sinclair was out having a round of golf and they were having difficulty contacting him. I really didn't care, I hadn't the strength to and I don't remember anything about the doctor arriving. My recollection of what followed is vague, one of rumbling along the long draughty hospital corridors to the endoscopy unit. Whether I was conscious all the time I'm not sure because I have very little recollection of that time. The next morning when I awoke, my first thoughts were of life. Realising I was still here I was half happy, half sad, and very, very low in every way. I had become so drained emotionally and physically that I had almost no reserves.

I wondered why no one phoned, or why Lynn hadn't been in. It was hard to understand this silence from home when I needed them so much. My strength gradually picked up, and it never ceased to amaze me how, after so much battering to my body, the healing process persistently sprang into action as an inbuilt instinct. During all the illness I had never lost my desire to eat and although swallowing had been difficult at times, I had always been able to eat enough to keep me going. I knew that my being alive was God's doing and that gave me new hope and courage to go on. The full purpose was not yet seen, but some things were being highlighted as time went by. Still I had to learn deep, deep lessons, and this was the only way to reach some of the hidden fears which lurked beneath the surface of my life, unseen and unchallenged until triggered off by recent events. There were many hard things to be faced yet, this my heart knew very well.

Eventually the nurses brought the mobile phone to me and I rang home and spoke to Ivan. He seemed to be very calm and as he spoke to me I soon discovered that nobody had told him how severe my last bout had been, and he was annoyed that he had not been contacted. Apparently Lynn had not been told either, but now that she knew she was back on hospital duty again. She was a blessing to me, but with her assignments due in soon, other pressures were on her. What a tower of strength she was, and oh, so welcome the sight her face and company. Sometimes her friends came in with her, along with others, but I was so weak this time I felt I needed some support from home. I was unable to stand and my food was just a liquid diet. Who could come? I began to plan in my head, and thinking it would be unsuitable for Ivan to come because of the kids, it was agreed that mum and dad would be the best just now. I felt it could be difficult for one person on their own to cope with because I knew they would be shocked when they saw me, and it's always good to have company when you are visiting hospital. Sometimes I think it is as hard on those visiting as it is on the person who is ill, as watching a loved one slowly deteriorate is a very painful thing.

My parents arrived, travelling light with an overnight bag. Little did they know what lay in store. By the time they came, my swallowing had become almost impossible, not that my desire for food had ceased, but all the treatment on the oesophagus to stop one problem, had caused another. Scars had formed in the oesophagus, causing infection and obstruction, and this was the reason I was no longer able to eat, absolutely nothing would go down. Dr. Sinclair was due around the day my folks arrived and when he came we were shocked to hear that he had decided to transfer me prematurely to Birmingham to be assessed for a liver transplant. I did not know what to think of this next turn of events, a liver transplant so soon had not been something I had expected.

At my original diagnosis, I was informed that I had fifteen to twenty years of good life in my liver. Because of this, I had expected to get progressively worse over the next 10 years, after which I would then need to consider a transplant as a last resort. Now, here I was, just 5 months after having been diagnosed, being sent prematurely to Birmingham to be assessed for a transplant. This was no small decision and it felt so sudden. I had no idea how I would be able to cope with this and wondered what the future held for me and my family. Was there to be much of a future anyway? Over these months of illness I had been contemplating the possibility of a transplant in the distant future but my quality of life had become such that, once again, I knew I had no choice in the matter if I wanted to live, and I did want to live. The zeal for life was very strong, much stronger than the few fleeting thoughts of death, especially because of how miraculously I had been kept during the last two episodes when I thought my time was up. One thing was certain, I certainly could not go to Birmingham alone. I was so weak I couldn't even stand and I couldn't eat or drink normally. After talking, we agreed that mum and dad would travel with me.

Although I was really weak, I never lost my sense of humour. Dad made me laugh because hospitals made him feel ill and tension in these situations often brought on sudden trips to the toilet, one of which took place just before we were ready to set off in the ambulance to the airport. I wondered aloud to mum if it would be safe to let dad go on his own, as the hospital was such a big place.

Off he set, sure that he knew where to go. Five minutes passed, then ten which grew to fifteen and still no return of father, by which time I was lying on the stretcher ready to go. I had felt sure he would get lost, which he had. He'd been given directions by some nurse on a totally different floor of the hospital and that's where the confusion arose. I had to laugh, what would they be like as guides to me in Birmingham if this was how it was in Aberdeen?

THE FLIGHT

It was March, 1991 and once again I was on a small plane awaiting clearance for take-off. My original fears of flying had vanished completely and it was a lovely day. The pilot of the little plane was very nice and the escort nurse was sensitive and efficient making us all feel at ease, except maybe dad, who hated flying as much as hospitals, especially a small plane like this. It's just as well I was unaware of this at the time, otherwise it may have caused me unnecessary tension worrying about him. It was amazing when the necessity arose, just how much each person involved rose to the new challenges and got the ability to cope.

It took most of the day to reach Birmingham and the flight was great although I was by no means feeling great. Looking down on our lovely country was wonderfully clear and I tried to pick out places as we went over. I spotted the Borders, the Lakes, and on the other side out towards the sea I thought I could see Blackpool. As we came in over Birmingham the houses seemed to go on for miles and miles and miles. BIRMINGHAM WAS BIG.

The ambulance men were there to meet us and our drive through the streets was hot. My first impression of Birmingham was how English all the houses looked. Red bricks, or whitewashed (painted) with dark wooden beams, bay windows and all the beautiful foliage. The magnolia trees were spectacular. We chatted with the ambulance man, who was very friendly and interested in where we came from. Dad was always keen for a yarn with anyone. After a long drive we eventually arrived at the Queen Elizabeth Hospital, and found it to be a massive place, four or five stories high and very old fashioned. I was wheeled along many corridors and up lifts, until we reached the Liver Unit where we were introduced to a male nurse named Peter, as well as others who looked after us. They found me a bed and got a welcome cup of tea for mum and dad.

My first day in the Liver Unit seemed so busy and I was surrounded by so many very ill people. Some looked really yellow and some almost green. One woman with a very puffed face and extremely swollen legs covered with tight stockings, seemed to be going home. I had thought she must be waiting for her transplant because she looked so awful that I appeared well in comparison.

The sun was beaming in through the huge window opposite me, as I struggled to adjust to the strangeness of the place and the strong Brummie accent. Hospitals are such alien places and I felt alone, cut off from home and anxious about the future. I felt ill, needy and weak but always deep down inside, my inner self in that area which is my soul, was very much alive. I hadn't lost my sense of God being in control and having a purpose in all this. I had always been able to read my Bible and pray and this was my main lifeline, the only familiar thing which created in me deep hope.

My parents had been given accommodation in a wing of the nurses' home called Nuffield House, a place made available for visiting relatives of hospital patients. It was very basic accommodation but a wonderful provision for people like mum and dad who had travelled so far and didn't know where or how to begin to look for a place to stay.

That first day, just after settling in, Edward Mason came to visit. Edward was a relative of my father who had spent a summer holiday with us at Howe the year before. He had been a missionary in Africa and had now come back to this country to do further training for ministry. He and his family were living in Bristol and Edward had received a call from my sister telling him that we were in Birmingham Q.E. and he had made the journey to see us .

He was a welcome sight, anything or anybody familiar in strange surroundings is so special. He brought thoughtful little things like worship tapes, women's magazines, a crossword book and his son's walkman. What a blessing these things were and the love with which they were brought touched my heart. Some of the songs on the tape are still a reminder to me of his kindness and how God used the words of these songs to keep me going through the loneliest and hardest of times. He took my folks out for a meal and I'm sure they were glad to have someone there who knew their way around and to take them out of the hospital atmosphere. By the time they came back I was able to swallow some nice cool iced milk drink, it took a long time but I managed.

THE ENDOSCOPY UNIT

The day after I arrived I went through the same old process of the 'nil by mouth' sign which had often hung over my bed in Aberdeen. Dr. Mutimer, a young Australian doctor and Dr. Davies, a young Welshman, were prominent in this unit. After inspection, they concluded that Dr. Sinclair had done a good job on the veins but the treatment had caused a lot of scarring and inflammation, so he prescribed a course of antibiotics and some anti acid drugs to stop ulcers forming.

I hated endoscopies, however they were very necessary things and they soon had me on the mend again. These two doctors were very special to me, they made me feel that I was a person with feelings, I felt that I mattered to them and they took time to talk to me about my disease and the treatment. They were reassuring and warm with a good sense of humour too, always ready for a laugh and I think of them fondly and with deep gratitude .

THE LIVER UNIT

The liver unit was a very specialised ward with a high dependency unit at one end where the most recently transplanted patients went after having come from intensive care elsewhere in the hospital. Next to that was the office on one side and the staff and store rooms across the corridor and to the right of the office was the liver unit, which consisted of a four bed ward first, for the most needy people, then an eight bed ward and beyond that another six bed ward. At the very end there was a sitting room for patients with a dining area, TV and video, games, etc. We were three stories up and therefore had a lovely view out over the city. Visiting times were long, which was great for me, beginning at 10.00 am to 1.30, then 3.00 to 8.00pm every day.

My bed was in the second ward. On the opposite side of the partition was a young boy whose name was Simon. He had suddenly developed an unusual liver disease and before it was properly diagnosed he had become seriously ill and was lying unconscious. His parents had signed the consent form for him to have a transplant and they were so pleased to see the good progress he was making. To me he looked so yellow although they thought he was doing so well, and really he was. It was ten days since his transplant operation and he was about to be discharged . As I looked at him I silently wondered if this could happen for me.

My father, being the natural protector, was not very happy about the fact that this Unit had mixed wards (male and female). He always made sure that my curtains were well pulled around me and at first I must say I found this a bit unusual myself, but I soon overcame any inhibitions realising that we were all in the same boat, so to speak, and being a mixed ward in many respects made life more normal and stimulated interesting conversations, creating more of a balance than a strictly male or female ward would have done.

Mum and Dad had made friends with lots of people, both patients and their families. Because of dad's friendly, outgoing personality he was soon able to get a conversation going. Simon's parents kept reassuring mum and dad that I must have a transplant as it would change my life. Across the ward from me was an old woman from Manchester who had the same disease as I did. She was frail and very pale and she kept bleeding internally and was undergoing assessment, too. Next to her, an older man had been admitted who looked really ill and was linked up to a drip constantly, while his wife looked anxiously on.

I must have slept soundly that night because in the morning I noticed the man had gone and I knew instantly that he had died in the night. When Mum and Dad came to visit they said his wife had been in Nuffield House too, and had been very upset by the sudden death of her husband. Living in hospital certainly brought me face to face with the reality of life and death. How fragile is this life of ours, again a reminder of how dependent we are on God. We cannot keep ourselves alive one minute unless God gives us breath.

Mum and dad stayed with me about a week and it was so helpful and comforting to have had them with me. Their love and care for me was truly special. They took me walks in a wheelchair, courageously managing the craziness of getting in and out of the lifts in time before the doors automatically closed. I had to be sure to keep my hands in, in case they got hurt. Mum was the chair driver and Dad the press button operator for the lift. How I loved getting out for a walk with the wind blowing in my face.

Long days, and during visiting times we had plenty of opportunity to talk. We did crosswords together, played scrabble and these things were all very necessary to keep my mind active and off myself. Always before bed time, Dad would read the Bible and say a prayer which was a great blessing to me. Times like these bring out the more sensitive side in all of us, and one night I was able to tell them how I believed God had told me that I would be healed by a transplant, however the practical outworking of this assurance was to be the most testing time so far in my entire life.

Mum and dad left giving me the assurance that I would never be without a friend to accompany me during my stay in England. This was Dad's major contribution to the next part of the story.

MY ASSURANCE FROM GOD

This assurance had come to me a long time before I knew anything about the present state in which I found myself. Because of my faith in God, I knew that nothing could happen to me that God did not already know about beforehand. I believed He loved me, was personally interested in me and was working things out in my life and although I couldn't always see this, I did believe it. Right back at the beginning, before I knew about my illness, God spoke to me from His word in Matthew chapter 10 v 28-31 *'but the very hairs of your head are all numbered, do not fear therefore, you are of more value than many sparrows'*. I knew I could trust God. I had been prayed for many times for healing at my own church and the Aberdeen church, but no divine healing came, so I had begun to ask God what His plans were for my life.

I sat on the edge of my bed there in Aberdeen one day at the start of all this, and asked God if He had a transplant in mind for my healing. I wanted to know if this was right, so in faith I prayed to ask that if it was to be so, that when the doctor did her rounds that morning she would say something specific about me getting a transplant although at that time she would not have had any real reason for saying it. That day, while on her ward round, she came and sat down on the side of my bed, tapped me on the leg and said right out of the blue, "Well, Mrs. Scott, what we would be looking for in the future is for you to have a transplant," and in my heart, I just knew that the Lord had prompted her to say that. I felt this was OK in my heart that God had said it through someone who had no idea what I was thinking, yet still I wanted Him to show me from His word that this was the way forward although I felt certain that the Bible did not contain any such proof for my situation.

One day as I sat reading my Bible, a passage just leapt out at me from Isaiah 43 v 1-7 but mostly verse 4. *'Since you are precious in My sight, You have been honoured, and I have loved you. Therefore I will give men for you and people for your life. Fear not for I am with you'.*

The Lord spoke to my heart again out of these verses of how much He loved me and how far He was prepared to go to restore my life and health to me. It spoke of how someone was going to have to die to give me life, so there it was in God's word, as if specially for me. Isn't it wonderful how God knows exactly what it takes to show us and when. Ordinarily, we should not pick parts of the Bible at random to make it say what we want, but that was not how it was. I knew that in order for me to have a transplant, someone was going to have to die and this was a very sobering thought and stark reality.

If this was true, then God knew all about it. Ps. 139 says He knew all about me before I was born, likewise everyone else in the world. Therefore, in His foreknowledge, He knew the person that was going to die at the very time I would need a transplant and whose liver I would receive that I might have life. Why? I don't know. Why would He want to do that for me? It could only be that my life has an unfinished purpose yet, I knew He had taught me lots about Himself already, but there was more. Now I was beginning to see some of the meaning of being here in Birmingham and believed God was with me, leading and directing events and working out my life according to His divine plan for me. With this knowledge I had to trust Him with every other area of my life and also my family, who were now even more distant from me. My home and church, my friends, my whole world had been turned upside down. Nothing was familiar except God and this I knew was the deep and lasting lesson He was teaching and I was slowly learning .

My family are His and His alone, not mine first, along with all the other things to which I had clung to give me security. The things I had built my life around and propped myself up with, the things I filled my life with to make me happy. These were all OK in their place, but they had all been given to me by God to look after for Him, to bless Him first and then me. Yes, He liked me to enjoy all these things, to find fulfilment in them, but they were not to take the first place which is His and His alone. My life was nothing without Him, my breath and very being is God given and when it's just me and Him nothing else matters. They have their place and each one is important, but at the end of our lives these things can't save us and what really counts whether I really know the Lord and His power in my life. At the end of my life will I be with him forever? Yes, I knew this was truth and His spirit in me was sustaining and breathing new life into me every day.

THE ASSESSMENT

Over the next weeks I would have to receive extensive assessment tests to see if I was a suitable recipient for a transplant. These tests included brain scans, heart monitoring, lung and breathing tests plus x-rays, kidney function tests and many, many blood tests. It seemed I was constantly being wheeled to or from one test to another and sitting in monotonous queues with other ill people, waiting for my turn. The tedium of staring at others more ill than myself, at people who were fixed up to drips and tubes and often with no conversation, just tiredness and illness as they constantly waited for the next test.

There was the added tension of not knowing how horrible it was going to be, and apprehensive thoughts of how long it would take and how uncomfortable it would be permeated the atmosphere. Because of the generally ill feeling, nobody felt like chatting or concentrating on reading. These tests continued on before and after mum and dad left. I looked forward to Ivan coming in a day or two because it had been many weeks since I had last seen him and I was longing to be with him again.

There was hope that I would be received on to the transplant programme fairly soon which meant the doctors needed to talk it over with my immediate family in order to explain all the various aspects of the operation and the possible complications, as well as giving us advice on alternative treatments should we decide to withdraw from surgery. Over phone calls we arranged the date for Ivan and all the family to come down.

At this time the three older children were due to come south to Ayr to a Christian holiday week called Spring Harvest '91 with my sister Helen and others from my church. They were to stop overnight on the way down with Muriel and George, distant relatives of my mother who lived in Alexandria near Glasgow. Mum had always kept the family ties with Muriel and she was very hospitable to any of the family who needed a bed, not to mention all the other lovely home comforts.

While my family were there, Muriel's daughter was up in Scotland also for an Easter break. Fiona lived in Wolverhampton, not far from the Q.E. where I was, and when she heard from the kids that I was there she decided she would come to see me when she returned home. After Spring Harvest, the family were to be joined by Ivan and James in Ayr and then travel south to Birmingham together by car. On the day they were due to arrive, I got the road atlas out of the sitting room to follow their progress, roughly working out where they would be at certain times of the day. It was a long day for me waiting and getting more and more excited at the thought of seeing them again. I was walking about now and getting stronger all the time, I was longing to see them although I would hardly allow myself to admit how much I missed them all.

Being constantly in hospital, I soon made friends with other patients. It's the common bond of understanding that comes from people who are either going through the same things as you or have already been through them and it gives such reassurance and great hope. Jenny Waterflood was one such person. She had been admitted into the bed next to me for her M.O.T as she called it, her annual review. It was three years since her transplant, she had a daughter the same age as our Sharon and a son the same age as our James. Her husband was a policeman and they were such a lovely, friendly family.

She shared with me how ill she had been before her op, showing me photos and a diary from that time when she'd had only a slim chance of pulling through. She was called in for surgery on Christmas Eve and she had never looked back since, and she mentioned that as soon as she came out of the anaesthetic she was on an unusual high which had stayed with her over the years.

As I looked at her healthy body, her lovely family, her illness and her courage, I felt a great hope. One of the positive sides to the liver unit certainly was seeing all those people coming back for check ups and looking so well. I wondered many times could this happen for me.

Jenny and her husband did all sorts of fund raising events to raise money for the Liver unit, including making lots of little clowns which she sold for £2.50 each. I had received a £10 note from a friend, which proved to be so timely because while in hospital it's surprising how often you need money and the little I did have with me had run out. I decided to spend it on clowns for the children, greatly desiring to be able to give them each something just to say I loved them and to let them know I cared for them. Somehow I hoped that this token gesture would be able to go toward making up for all the things I was unable now to do for them.

As I looked out from the hospital window I could see the canal just behind the railway line. Nearer to me was the huge clock tower of the university. The canal intrigued me as I had never seen long boats before and it amazed me just how many would move along there in a day. I felt it strange to see something so rural in the centre of the city.

Maybe it's because it was the only thing in this vast expanse of streets and houses that remotely resembled the country that it attracted my attention so or maybe it was the sheer freedom it represented that stirred that sense of longing to be out there and free. Now it was late in the evening and I had expected them much sooner.

I had walked the corridor just outside the Liver unit many times that day looking, waiting, longing. I was staring down across the car park towards Nuffield House, deep in thought, when someone called my name. I looked up, startled, and there they were. What a sight. My heart was pounding, and smiling, I choked back the tears to enjoy the hugs, smiles and everybody talking at once. It was a feeling of sheer joy and satisfaction at seeing this special, lovely family of mine. Being with them was better than any medicine. It showed me how much we all need that tender loving care and the feeling of loving and being loved. How I had missed Ivan, much, much more than I could cope with expressing. The truth was, that in order to survive, I had to suppress a lot of the feelings, otherwise I would have spent most days crying. I'm not sure that I really did work this out at the time. I thought I was coping very well but later it became apparent that this was a necessary reaction at the time in order to survive from day to day.

I know Ivan was having his own feelings and stresses which I knew nothing about either and so he had to suppress too, in order for him to be able to exist on his own. At the time you just have to get on with living and coping with the situation you find yourself in as best you can. Ivan's work was a great help for him, a complete switch off from the reality of the missing and the pain and loneliness inside. Maybe one day he will be able to share his own thoughts, too. Ivan was a constant source of strength for me. He gave me a reason for living, knowing he was always there for me kept me going. He was undoubtedly good for the heart condition. Our hearts so cry out for love but when the body is caught up with illness and our attention is focused on that it's so easy to forget that we are emotionally pining for love, comfort, gentle reassurance and a sense of belonging. We all need a place where our heart feels secure, with someone to lean on and support us, a person to hold our hand and tell us it will be all right. For me, that person was Ivan.

The next few days with the family were so special and we had lots to talk about, Lynn's exams coming up soon and Sharon's highers. They had their own pressures and an ill mother on top of all that, but I was pleased at how well they seemed to be coping. It was so good to see their faces and talk and laugh together. Jonathan was very quiet and thoughtful, while James, as I look back, was such a little boy, but he was so good and seemed fine too. Drawing was one of his favourite pastimes and it was a good way of amusing himself during these long days of hospital visits which was so out of the ordinary for all of them. I presented them with their little clowns and it was fun to be able to surprise them with a present from mum, especially since shopping was not one of my most regular habits in recent months. This special treat was meant to bless them and it did and they still have those clowns after all these years.

I was still going through the final tests for assessment and one day over the visit we were to have a talk with Dr. Nuburger about all the risks involved. We needed to be informed of both the dangers and the benefits so that we could make a knowledgeable decision. The chat went well and he emphasised several times that although the operation might go OK many other things could go wrong. There was a possibility of developing complications after transplant, such as liver rejection, etc. I wasn't really afraid of dying, it was more how I died that bothered me. I think we all have ways that we would prefer to go, given the choice. Under anaesthetic, I thought, would be very painless compared to the idea of complications after going through it all. Nevertheless, I had no other choice than to have the op if my life was to continue, because the threat of death was imminent in my everyday life. The only alternative offered to me was a shunt, which meant just as big an op, diverting the blood flow out of the liver causing the veins to stop bursting, but to still have the disease and deteriorating health had serious risks too, and held no appeal to me.

All the tests were successful and I was accepted on to the transplant list to await a suitable donor. Every other part of my body was healthy apart from my liver and this was in my favour. Many people I had met over the time had been assessed and not accepted for various reasons, such as weak hearts, lungs or kidneys. I felt really relieved to be on the list. I signed all the papers and I was told that for my particular blood group I was third on the waiting list. I was given a bleeper to carry with me at all times should a liver become available.

We decided that I should stay down in that area because to go all the way back to Orkney was too risky for various reasons. We were told it could be weeks or months to wait but we had a certain peace that it might not be that long. Up until now, my family had all been able to stay in Nuffield House but now they needed to move out to give room for others and I was to be discharged from hospital too, which posed another problem. We had no idea where we would find a place to stay. We did not know where to even begin to look in a strange place and the cost of B&B alone would be an incredible expense for all of us. While I was having my mid-day nap, Ivan set off to find a place. I prayed and asked the Lord to help them find somewhere easily and, as I lay there in a slight slumber, I heard footsteps coming towards my bed and a cheery little voice greeting me. Fuddled by sleep I wondered who on earth this pretty lady was.

"Do you not know me?" she asked. Oh, this was Fiona, Muriel's daughter whom my kids had met on their way to Ayr. It was so nice to see her, she looked so smart and smiley and little did either of us know that she was going to be part of God's wonderful provision for me over this next difficult stage. Talking together, Fiona kindly offered hospitality to any of the family while they were down saying we could come and stay anytime. At that precise moment she had no idea what she was offering or the long term effects of her kind gesture, but I'm sure she was sent to us that day and as a family we will be eternally grateful for her generous heart. Her visit was short and sweet, she gave me her address and phone number and off she went.

I was so excited to tell Ivan when he got back that day that I had got accommodation for them. He was surprised at how easily this poorly woman had found a place to stay. Again God was showing us how He was always one step ahead of our needs. They went off to Fiona's for the night and the next day I was discharged.

The family thought it was great that I would be getting out while they were down but for me it was more than a bit scary. Being discharged in a strange place, imposing on other people's hospitality, using their home and invading their privacy, all these fears welled up in me. I was the kind of person who loved to have folks in my home, eating my food, being cared for by me and I felt it so difficult allowing myself to receive from Fiona what I loved to do for others so freely.

Fiona and Rob Dawson had a little girl called Emma, a delightful one year old who spent every day at a local nursery while her parents continued in full time employment. Rob was a lawyer who worked in Walsall, and Fiona was a manageress working for a firm who supplied hospitals with a variety of different goods. She was a very responsible business woman, they were both professional people who also enjoyed a busy social life. They were a delight to be with and if they felt we were a nuisance, it definitely wasn't obvious. I instantly liked them both. Fiona was a gourmet cook and it wasn't safe to say I liked something or I could guarantee she would buy it. I couldn't swallow any lumpy food and everything had to be liquidised. Nothing ever seemed to be any bother to her and she was so kind to me that it touches my heart still as I write.

THE WOLVERHAMPTON EXPERIENCE

Alpine Way in Compton was to be my home base for the next stage, and I wondered how long that would be. It felt odd being out and trying to be a normal mum in such abnormal circumstances, however I was making an effort for the children's sake. We went for short walks in the parks and enjoyed the squirrels, a novelty for Orcadians. I didn't have much energy and strength but my family had so much and wanted to go places and do things that I just didn't have the heart for.

Edward and Hilary Mason lived not too far away, in Bristol, so we decided to go there on a day trip travelling down the motorway and spending a lovely day with their family and rounding off the end of the day with a lively game of football. It was good to see them all having such good fun. Bristol was nice but just another city and not much like the wide open spaces I was used to in Orkney. How I longed for the keen, strong wind blowing in my hair instead of the choking smell of car fumes, rushing traffic and the jungle of houses and so many people of every colour and class which was certainly a culture shock for me. I was amazed at how many Asian people lived in Wolverhampton. Coming from a small island community it was hard for me to adjust to the fact that our country has changed so much. In the parks, most of the kids were Asian and most of the older people sitting on the park benches were Asian too. There was no prejudice in my heart, it was just so different.

COMPTON

It didn't take long to find our way around this area and the street itself had about thirty nine houses, all the same with open front gardens. Across the road was a piece of waste ground with an old farm house and barn in need of repair. It had originally been an orchard but the previous owner had pulled up all the trees so now all that remained were weeds and poppies. Because this land was between our street and the main road into the city centre, the traffic noise was reduced greatly. At the back of the house there was a huge 15 ft cliff which ran the length of the street. It was a wonderful feature in the garden, overhung as it was with a variety of trees and plants. At the bottom of the cliff Rob had made a rockery with a patio in front of it which made it a beautiful place for barbecues. The back garden was a very safe place for little Emma to play as there was no escape, it was completely closed in by the garage and the house and a tall dividing fence between each garden. The washing line and the garden shed were out there, too. The house itself had four upstairs bedrooms and a bathroom, with a living room downstairs at the front with a lovely bay window and a dining room off that with a conservatory beyond it, opening on to the back garden. The kitchen looked out on the back as well and through the kitchen was the garage which opened out into the back garden, too. The whole house was very tastefully decorated, everything matched beautifully with lots of Laura Ashley stuff. We occupied the bedrooms at the back and from there we had a great view of the other gardens.

We found a beauty spot just beyond the houses, which we could get to by walking down under an old railway bridge towards the canal or walking up over it to take a leisurely stroll through the majestic trees. These walks were always busy with people.

Down by the canal for me was a completely new concept, we would often stop and chat to others while watching the long boats pass through the lock gates. The whole operation of these locks was fascinating and seemed such a relaxing way to spend a holiday. On the other side of the canal a man had set up a boat building business. In talking with him, he said that a new long boat would cost about £40,000 and some people would sell their houses to buy one and live permanently on them. My sister Rosalind once said she didn't fancy waking up every morning with nothing but water underneath her. At the end of the path along the canal we had to cross the main road to reach the small local shopping centre. There was a little inn there which became a place to escape to occasionally when we needed to get out and also to give Rob and Fiona a bit of peace. We found folks in the area so friendly and eager to speak, not at all as I had imagined they would be .

The shopping centre had a chemist, drapery, supermarket, post office, dry cleaners, chip shop and take away plus a hairdresser and newsagent, so really it had everything I needed. The traffic going through Compton was unbelievable and even worse at rush hour. It seemed strange that just beyond the road there was a lovely country spot in the middle of Wolverhampton, kept just for me, or so I felt. It was such a touch of home for me, with the birds and the fish, the smells and the delicate flowers. It felt as though God had placed me here and all my smallest needs were being met.

PAINFUL PARTINGS

I wasn't looking forward to Ivan and the family leaving, although I knew they had to go. It had been so good for me to have seen them all again, to feel like a mum, to love and be loved. To act almost normal was such a blessing. The day they left is so vivid in my memory as we all sat on the big double bed in our room and, as was the custom at any parting, we prayed together blessing each other and asking the Lord to keep us safe until we met again. As we prayed, some of us soon became very emotional. I'm never very good at controlled partings when everything is going fine, let alone the way things were with us now. All the suppressed feelings, fears and pains were beginning to come to the surface and each of us strove to handle it our own way. We could only express a very small part of this in our prayer time, but on the other hand, it was good to be faced with the reality of our hearts' pain, deep down inside. It's often only at times like this that these places are touched.

At the time, it seemed to me that Jonathan looked quite indifferent about the whole thing, which hurt since we had been pretty close before my illness, and I challenged him about his attitude. It's so strange to realise that when these feelings go unchallenged we can actually convince ourselves we are coping all right, believing a lie and appearing so together on the surface but with a pain inside that is too awful to face. I suppose we all felt a bit like that but were not so good at disguising it Once we spoke about it, it was apparent that he was as sore as the rest of us but was trying to be brave. Jonathan and I had always been very good friends, I just knew how he ticked and we had a mutual respect and understanding. I didn't prefer him to any of the others, it was just the way things were. Consequently, when I had suddenly been removed from his life, it had become increasingly difficult for me to have any depth of relationship with him and he seemed to be missing that more than the rest. Every stage of growing up is hard, even with both parents around to love and care and most difficult in these early teenage years. It was getting to him and no wonder, I was so caught up with me and it was increasingly hard to pick up from where we had left off last time. No matter how much we would all have liked things to be the same, they could never be. I couldn't really share my innermost fears with them, I didn't really know if things would ever be the same again and I was almost scared to believe I would ever be the person I used to be. I even wonder if I really wanted to be, it seemed I didn't know any more.

There were times when I would rather that God had taken me home that first night on the sofa, because the reality of working out the difficulties and obstacles on a day to day basis was becoming a very painful experience. As I look back over that time, I can see I coped in my own way. I decided not to let myself feel all the things that upset me but set my mind to accept things as they were, knowing that I was unable to change the things that were happening to me. I endeavoured to continue to be grateful for every material and physical blessing and not think too much on home and family, church and Orkney. Because of praying together in the company of my family, these feelings were not easily controlled or hidden for they represented everything I tried to close out.

Jonathan, a mere 14 years old, was maybe feeling more than the rest of us. Early teenage years for a youth are so sensitive and important and there is already so much going on in their own lives to handle without the added complication of a seriously ill mother. It was small wonder that he had become more distant. We all prayed and cried together, dreading the parting. Outside we had lots of hugs as I choked back the tears, but the lump in my throat turned to tears as I waved them all goodbye. Only God knew if I would ever see them again in this life. I felt lonely, sad and afraid as I continued to cry. That day Fiona had arranged for her next door neighbour to sit with me until the next lot of family back up arrived. Maureen was chatty and friendly and worked as a part time assistant in the local Marks and Spencers while her husband was a lecturer at a local Polytech. Their son and daughter were very grown up and the girl was very motivated and glamorous. The family had a golden labrador which was very well behaved and always under control. Maureen was good company for the day and I appreciated Fiona's thoughtfulness in making sure I had someone to talk to, especially having just said goodbye to my family.

The family had planned to travel up to Aberdeen and Lynn was a great help with the driving although their trip was complicated by the sick bug Sharon had caught. A sick bug on the motorway isn't quite as simple as pulling into the side of a country road in Orkney, but they laugh about it now. It's my experience that dads are not as good as mums at handling sick kids. I was just glad they hadn't left the bug with me.

My dad had arranged for my sisters, Rosalind and Vera to come down and stay. They travelled by boat to Scrabster then bus to Inverness, with an overnight stop there and by train to Birmingham the next day. I was excited about seeing them and it gave me something to look forward too. These visits from the family were so important in order for me to retain a positive attitude and bring the reality of my home life closer. It gave me the hope and reassurance I needed during my exile in England.

Next door on the other side of Fiona's was another lovely couple, Liz and Larry, who had taken me into their hearts. She was Scottish and he was Indian and they had four beautiful children ranging in ages from 24 - 14. Toscha, the oldest, was full time with the Salvation Army, then Lara, Liza and John the youngest. He was the same age as Jonathan and he and I hit it off almost immediately, he would often pop into Fiona's for a chat and ask how I was. The kindness and hospitality this family showed to me was heart warming and at times invaluable. Their dog, Baldrick, was everything that Maureen's wasn't. He was naughty, he barked, jumped up on you, ran off, occasionally bit people, chased Fiona's cat, etc. etc. Liz was very good with her hands, sewing and doing creative, arty things. She was a homely, warm, motherly person with a great sense of humour. Maybe I liked her because she spoke my language. Larry had an executive job so they were well off but he had a weekend taxi service too, and I noticed again how hard Asian people are prepared to work .

Coming from a small island community where everybody knows everybody, I had the idea that nobody knew who their next door neighbour was here in the south, but this place blew that idea apart. This street had such a friendly neighbourhood who really took an interest in each other with a genuine concern.

A SISTER'S SURVIVAL KIT

Rosalind and Vera arrived just before I was due to go into the Q.E. Hospital again for another briefing on the op. I still had a few doctors to talk to and my veins needed to be checked again. The doctors had talked about getting the opening into my stomach stretched since with all the treatment it had narrowed, making swallowing difficult .

It was special having Rosalind and Vera with me for company and spiritual encouragement, we had some good prayer times and some good laughs too. One day on a trip to the shops with Fiona, I had seen a huge banner hanging outside a church called Wolverhampton Christian Fellowship, so when Sunday came we asked Fiona if she would mind us going to the church. She took us and picked us up. It was very similar to our church at home, they were friendly and caring and took a great interest in us and prayed for me in the meeting. It was lovely and as we left they asked us to remind them when I went in for the transplant so that they could pray for me.

This time I was not admitted to the Liver Unit, I was in another ward which often took the surplus patients. It was another strange place with new nurses, but the same doctors treated me. At first I was in a little two bedded side room but I was the only one in it and time dragged on so much, with no one to talk to for hours. Nevertheless, visiting times were much longer than the other hospitals I had been in. Rosalind and Vera were staying in Nuffield House in the family wing provided. They were pretty scared of being attacked, especially in the tunnel provided underneath the road, connecting the hospital to Nuffield House. It was there for the protection of the nurses going across to the nurses' home when they went off duty so that they wouldn't need to go outside on their own. It was ideal, but to two Orcadian women, unaccustomed to the threat of attack, anybody, anywhere was a potential attacker. However, they had their means of self protection just in case their fears became a reality. Thankfully they never needed to put it to the test.

Rosalind once said that she would hate to be me and she didn't know how I could manage so well. My answer was that I would much rather be here in this warm hospital being cared for in every way than be a Kurd refugee walking barefoot in freezing conditions across the hills to freedom, with no food or medicine or any cover from the weather. I had a warm bed, clean sheets, food, love and everything that could possibly be done was being done for me. I felt privileged and special. Ill and weak, but special. Why was my life being preserved in this way?

After my treatment, the stretching had caused a bleed again, so they needed to keep a close eye on me for the next few hours. I woke up in a completely different ward and having no idea where I was. Apparently, after they had done my endoscopy, they had seen lots of veins in my stomach were about to burst. Rosalind and Vera were not enjoying this experience very much, but having them with me was so comforting. I knew they had made a sacrifice to come down, leaving their young families who had never been without them for any reason apart from having a baby. So for them, too, it was difficult leaving and coming to be with me. I will be eternally grateful for every sacrifice made by every member of my family for me, so that I could be blessed.

I had to see the anaesthetist and Dr. Padbury and visit the High Dependency Unit (H.D.U.) After transplant, I would go to the I.T.U. first, then to the H.D.U. which was joined to the Liver Unit. This was not a scary experience for me because by now I had seen so many seriously ill people at all the different stages, but for my sisters it was pretty daunting and I suppose they couldn't help but be aware that soon this would be happening to me. Now we were seeing patients right after transplant with tubes, bleepers and drips everywhere, along with charts, nurses, etc. There were five beds in this unit and I noticed an Asian woman in particular who had charms and faces of gods all round her bed. She looked very ill and her idols were obviously doing her no good because she looked awful. We were glad to get out.

Dr. Padbury was an Australian in England, learning new skills for the transplant programme back home. He was a super doctor and I had seen him a few times already on the ward rounds. He seemed warm and caring and was keen to talk, excellent with the patients. He was here to explain some of the final arrangements since he would be taking part in my surgery. He was very interested in Orkney and asked lots of questions, including if we had dingos there. Our Orcadian dialect amused him and we made it clear to him that we were trying very hard to speak good English so that he would understand us better. I liked him, he treated me as if I mattered and it seemed he cared about the whole person. I didn't feel like just an experiment to him.

Back at Fiona's we were more relaxed again, it was so nice to be in a home. Fiona's job meant she spent a lot of her working day driving from one appointment to another and sometimes she was away overnight, depending how far she had to travel. Rob was fairly late getting back most nights so it meant that we were in the house on our own all day. We would often have Rob's dinner cooked when he got back and one night we were to have pork chops so the sisters got to work on the meal. Rosalind, with her keen sense of smell, was convinced that the pork was off, so after much discussion it was decided that for the sake of my health the meat was not fit to eat. It was dumped in the bin and some other exotic dish was cooked up. Rob and Fiona duly arrived home ready for their pork treat, only to find it dumped. Fiona was amazed that the meat was off and slightly hurt, but it was too late. The kitchen door opened on to the garage where the bin was kept so Rob and Fiona set about checking out the meat for themselves and we were soon to discover that the cat had retrieved the pork out of the bin and had dragged it across the garage floor and was munching away happily at the smelly chop. I was very embarrassed, since I had always tried to be tactful and considerate, trying hard not to get in the way or to take advantage of their extraordinary kindness. When Rob had checked out the meat he said it wasn't off at all and the smell was only the kidney which had been packed with it, and you can imagine the powerful smell coming off the chops. We only had a few such embarrassing moments like that over the months which I hope they have forgiven us for. We deserved a good telling off for our cheek.

Vera and Rosalind slept in the small room at the back next to mine, but I suggested that they move into mine. This may have seemed strange to Fiona who was an only child and therefore hadn't enjoyed the fun of having real sisters which is what we were, although I felt Fiona was now adopted into the family too. For us it was great fun with a real sense of being family.

Vera and I slept in the double bed, we were very careful to keep to our own side and we all knew we would have given anything to have been sharing the bed with our own men, but that was impossible so we made the most of the time together. It reminded me of times when we were growing up together, a lot of girls in the same room talking and laughing into the night and sharing the same bed. I wonder now-a-days where all the sense of good clean family relationships have gone wrong and even where they are clean, they can be made to seem wrong. It all seems so sad. I slept next to the window, we joked that this was the sleeping order because if a burglar came in the window he would get me first and since I was in poor shape anyhow it wouldn't matter. The little room was packed but it was so nice to have their constant company and they stayed with me almost two weeks.

There was always the continuous flow of letters and cards from home, some from folks I didn't even know. They were all an endless supply of strength to me and kept me in touch with folks there. Some made me laugh, some made me cry, I still have them all, wonderful memories. My nieces and nephews and friends' children sent lovely little drawings and notes to cheer me up, which they did. Children have that unique way of touching the heart. I didn't reply to everyone who wrote but I did regularly write my close family and friends. I would write separate letters to my children, just to let them know they were all individually thought of and I would buy little things from the shops to send them, too.

MAY, 1991   FOREVER FAMILY

I had met a lot of Fiona's friends and family by now, and one of these was Rob's mum, Jean Dawson. She was a lovely little lady and she had come over to stay with me until the next batch of my relatives arrived. Jean lived in a town nearby and she led a very active life, had her own car and was interesting company. She took me on drives and shopping trips to local places like Codsall, where I found a super little craft shop to feed my appetite for

81

cross stitch. Jean also looked after little Emma one day a week and I went out with them sometimes.

The next to travel down were mum and Jennifer, my oldest sister. They flew to Aberdeen and then on to Birmingham. It had been a long time since I had seen Jennifer, although I had enjoyed her letters which were always light and often amusing. It was a joy to see them both, it made my heart glad. Mum always had a worried look about her probably because it makes no difference what age we are, our parents are still concerned for us. A mother is a very special person and I felt mine was extra special. A mother always loves, always cares, always hopes and a mother never stops being a mother. What a comforting thought.

In the same way, a sister never stops being a sister and Jennifer had always been my big sister. She was more confident in travelling than mum and had come to look after her and me. The same sleeping arrangements were adopted for the duration of their stay. Nothing too dramatic happened when they were down. Jennifer was an expert at the crosswords and we often went for walks by the canal and up to the shops, remembering to keep my bleeper handy in case of a quick call from the hospital. Jennifer worked in the kitchen of the local school and had to ask time off to accompany Mum. All of this mattered to me. I knew it cost people money and valuable time which they probably didn't have to spare, but they did it anyhow for me. They will never know how much these visits meant to me, they were to me a lifeline which kept home a living part of me. Being constantly cut off from home made it become distant and far away, but the steady stream of folk from home kept me in touch.

We had come to the end of another week and Jennifer was ready for home. Birmingham proved to be a very difficult and expensive place to fly to and from. To get a connecting flight to take them home to Orkney the same day they needed to leave Fiona's at 5 am to get the right train from Wolverhampton to Birmingham airport and we often found the trip was plagued with delays.

In order of age my family was Jennifer, Moira, Helen, Rosalind, Carolyn, Jimmy, Vera and so far three of them had been down. Cally, my younger sister, was next. She had never gone such a distance on her own before and up to now, she had been the only one to do so. I don't think I would have managed on my own but full praise to Cally, she showed us all up by arriving alone and on time. We were so glad to see her. She and Mum appeared constantly worried. Cally was closest to Fiona in age and because Fiona's family had often spent family holidays in Orkney, Cally and Rosalind had entertained Fiona with the Orcadian night life and wonderful hospitality. They had great fun catching up on old times and seemed to have a lot in common.

While Cally was down, we three went on frequent shopping trips during which Fiona bought lots of stylish outfits for her work. She was a very smart dresser and being petite, she always looked good. Wee Emma had some stunning little outfits too. She was the apple of her father's eye and he was so good with her. She was a little treat for me at this time and she took to me very quickly. She was at the sitting stage so she couldn't move around on her own yet. I had been to her nursery a few times when picking her up. It was a modern well equipped nursery, ideal for her. It was amazing how many of these nurseries were around, it has become a very acceptable part of parenting these days, not at all what I had been accustomed to, but such is the way of life in our modern society. Emma was happy and this was normal life for her. Fiona was a great hostess, cook, entertainer and I was so glad to be part of their home during the time I was there. Even though they were so busy, they made me and my family very welcome.

I was feeling better all the time now, and on the weekend that Cally was down, Rob and Fiona took us on a trip to a place called Ironbridge, a pretty little English town beside the river Severn with a very steep road running through the town and a strong iron bridge across the river. It was beautiful and teeming with visitors because the bridge was a tourist attraction. We got out and went for a walk. It was a hot sunny day and fairly hard going for me to walk up the steep hill, but I made it. We walked back down and went for a cup of tea and cakes at a little cafe. This was a memorable day for me of the type which I hadn't had too much of recently. This town held special memories for Fiona and Rob because it was where Rob had proposed to her, so this was a sentimental journey for them. They had only been married a couple of years so they were still adjusting to each other's lifestyles and coping with a continuous flow of strangers through their home. They were wonderful people .

On returning home that night I felt a bit weary and, knowing all the telltale signs, I realised I'd had a bleed again. Mum and Cally looked stressed as I phoned the Q.E. and I was, too. Off we set on another excursion to Birmingham with Fiona driving us and I was admitted to the Liver Unit. It was the weekend and I was unable to have immediate treatment because I was not an emergency. The endoscopy doctor that night was a thin faced, mean looking man, and as he looked, so he was. He couldn't really be bothered with me and it was clear that I was a nuisance. He was rude and hurtful which I assumed was just because it was the weekend and it was only me that he was annoyed with, but on talking to other patients later, I found this was apparently pretty normal behaviour for him. It was a relief to know that it wasn't just me.

Sometimes during endoscopies, I became aware of what they were doing although they didn't realise that. The drug they gave me should have had the effect of taking away my awareness but still leaving me able to obey commands while under it. Perhaps they hadn't given me quite enough but I knew there was a huge cumbersome thing down my throat. I remember being sick and trying to pull the thing out and the few times this happened it was very unpleasant and scary. This time it proved to be a small ulcer which had formed since they last looked so that was a relief.

I had been admitted to the first section of the Liver Unit where all the most ill or recently transplanted patients were. I had a big man on my right who had come through a recent operation, he was quite young and looked very yellow. I remembered the man opposite me from my assessment days, he was tall and skinny with very spotty skin, a serious expression and his legs were a mess. I realised now that the first day I had seen him, he had come in for his transplant. It looked as if he was coming on well now. That night after mum and Cally left me to go to Nuffield House, a woman in the H.D.U. died. I guessed it was the Asian woman I had seen in there when I had been shown round.

Those people can certainly mourn. Someone from the family began to wail and it was fearful and bloodcurdling. I had never heard anything like it before. Hospital life certainly brought me face to face with death. No wonder this poor family wailed. Their false religion gave them no peace, no life and in death, such pain that I could almost feel. I didn't know what to do and so I cried out to my God. The man in the bed next to me was very bothered by the noise and I started to talk to him. His name was Colin and he said he had been in the H.D.U. with the woman and was shocked by her death. His wife was over in Nuffield House too and he was a farmer, so we had that in common. He had suffered from the same illness as I had, only they had just caught him before his veins exploded. The doctors told him he was like a walking time bomb. Although he didn't give much in conversation, I enjoyed chatting away to him, anyhow.

Later on that night, his buzzer went and he couldn't get to sleep. He wasn't the only one. The upset of the woman's death had clearly shaken him. I overheard him talking to the nurse wanting to know that they would call his wife anytime during the night if anything went wrong. They spent some time reassuring him but during the night he developed a terrible back pain and was restless all night with doctors moving to and fro. I'm sure that it was absolute fear that started the back pain off, but I'm no doctor. They found no medical reason for it, which to me seemed strange. All in all, it was a disturbed night

In the morning mum and Cally arrived on time, oblivious to all the happenings of the night. It was just as well they were gone before the wailing started because hospitals had the same effect on Cally as they did on dad. She hated them and they made her feel ill too. She didn't know how I could stay so cool. Maybe to others looking at me it seemed that way. I felt pretty cool as this had now become a way of life to me. It was now normal and sometimes I felt more secure in hospital than out in the big wide world.

A very dear friend of mine, Gill Fraser from Orkney, was down in Leeds visiting her family so she was able to come to see me as well. She and her husband had moved to Orkney a few years before the Orkney Christian Fellowship started and we had become close friends in the church over the years, having a mutual respect and love for each other. She had been wanting to come and see me for a while and had never been fitted into dad's rota of visitors, not deliberately but there were certain times which suited her which often clashed with family. In times of sickness, families can become quite possessive and protective of their loved ones, and they have a great desire to do something to help and the visits were just that but sometimes to the exclusion of other friends. I would gladly have had anyone and everyone who cared to come. Gill arrived that day and it was a real joy to see her. Her timing was perfect too. Her eyes spoke volumes as she scanned the ward. Seeing all the yellow people and my obvious deathly appearance must have been dreadful, especially to someone who had not seen me for months. I must have looked awful and because I had become progressively ill, I didn't notice the decline as clearly as others who hadn't seen me for a long time.

I valued Gill's friendship dearly. She had taken on all the ironing for my family. Who can ever repay such acts of kindness, it's as well that the Lord keeps count of them all as I lost count a while ago. Gill just came for the day and went back up to Leeds the same day, and she was such good company for me and mum and Cally. I wished I could have had more good of her but it wasn't to be this time. Cally was glad to get out of that place the next day and go back to Fiona's.

I made an appointment to get my hair permed and mum came with me. It was a bit of a laugh really because I had to carry my bleeper everywhere with me. As I sat contentedly waiting for the perm to take, I heard what I thought was the bleeper going off. I panicked. What would I do, half permed? All of a sudden it stopped. It was a false alarm, only the timer which had been set for someone else in the hairdressers. It was such a fright. There had been some doubt anyhow as to the workings of the bleeper as I had accidentally dropped it in a plate of rather thick soup and so the bleep had become a bit garbled.

THE HEART AND SOUL OF A FAMILY

Mum and Cally were due to leave, to be replaced by Ivan. Right now he was in the middle of the lambing season, the busiest, most tiring time of the farming year for him. Poor Ivan, and I wasn't there to be any support to him. I thought of him often and longed to see him again. During these long nights sitting up in the lambing with plenty of time to think, Ivan put pen to paper and wrote me some very touching letters which always made me greet (cry). I could almost hear his voice as I read them and my throat choked with emotion. He had his own sense of humour, too, and often his letters would contain peedie fun things that he knew would amuse me. I was so desperately looking forward to seeing him again, he was the person I longed to see most of all and I missed him the most too. Not only to be there for me, but because I loved his company. We had a special friendship above all else and I missed that terribly.

Ivan was to travel down by plane to Edinburgh and then on to Birmingham and Cally had given him the benefit of some of her travel expertise. Being a lone traveller, she had found out some useful phrases like 'press for pod'. Apparently the pod was a small train service from the plane to the station which, if you got the right connections, eventually took you to the University station near the Q.E. and also, if you caught other connections, it took you right to Wolverhampton. He couldn't go wrong according to Cally, and he didn't.

IVAN'S VISIT

I was so excited about seeing Ivan again after all this time. Fiona had arranged for her next door neighbour, Maureen, to come in and keep me company. We had no problem sharing conversation that day and I always appreciated Fiona making all these thoughtful little arrangements for me.

I was sitting at the window watching for Ivan when the taxi arrived. What a joy to see him again, he always looked so fit and healthy and he was nicely tanned after the lambing. We were going to make the most of our three weeks together. Catching up on all the home news and just taking time to be with each other, something which had become all too stifled by illness and circumstance, we now had caught a little space to call our own. We spoke lots, went for food, watched TV, walked and it was so good to hear all the news.

Helen and Cally were on clean up duty at Howe, Sharon looked after the washing for the whole family and cooked and cleared up the kitchen, she was brilliant at doing her bit. I know, just by being a mum, how much of these little everyday things go unnoticed in the daily running of the home and when mum's there, nobody really bothers much because it is just expected to be done and it is. In reality, it's an awful lot of work, the shopping alone for a big family takes considerable thought and time. Sharon was no doubt taken for granted, but she nevertheless coped well in the face of it. Jonathan did his share of cooking and he was good at it too, so all in all, Ivan was well looked after. The pressures on my husband must have been immense, but like many men, he was rather good at burying his feelings and coped by keeping busy. I believe it was important for him to do that, and it was so easy to get lost in work with a big farm to run. It meant that if he chose to, he could almost spend 24 hours every day and still never come to the end of all that needed to be done. It was always more a case of getting the essentials done every day, because a day never seemed to be long enough, especially in the spring on a farm. The pressure of work is incredibly heavy with calving, lambing, land work, manure spreading and slurry, not to mention all the animal husbandry needed with young animals. There was plenty of opportunity for Ivan to lose himself in his work.

However, even with all the work and underlying worry and stress of my illness, it was obvious God was doing a deep work in him, too, that nothing else but what we were going through could have done. This was true for all of us. We were all being stretched to the limit in every way, but these strange and unusual circumstances were maturing us, and making us grow up so much. We all knew that with God there are endless resources and we were certainly drawing from them in order to be able to keep going.

I observed people over this time and it became obvious that there were those without the knowledge of God in their lives, who had such an inner drive to go on living and others who were the opposite. I'm no psychologist but it seemed to me that these inner attitudes seemed to already be there in a person, either as a positive or negative response to the same problem and it's not necessarily anything to do with God, it's just the way we are. Still, I do believe that with the knowledge of God inside a person, even a negative person, God can draw in alongside that person's normally negative reactions and change the way they would naturally react, thus finding faith and hope in an otherwise hopeless situation. This involves changing the person's mind and creating life from within. Only God can do that. I know, because I am by nature a pretty negative person, and I don't know how I would have been able to hold out with my own reserves to keep positive because they just weren't there. It was the knowledge of God from within me that kept me going and this my soul knows very well. This concept of a God knowing all my inmost thoughts, fears and worries, my every need, hopes and dreams totally and completely, and who was interested in me personally was wonderful to me. More and more I was discovering how to put my faith in God into practice, my faith and belief in God as not just a distant remote being up in the sky, but a real, live, ever present, living friend, helping me in every way, every day.

Gradually over the years leading up to my illness, many situations had arisen where I had felt the Lord had been preparing me very gently and gradually for what I was now experiencing, but at the time all these little lessons in trust and faith were not so obvious as they were now, and so I could see so much more clearly the purpose of some of the events that had taken place years before.

I had always found it very hard to leave the children with anyone else since I felt that nobody else could look after them as well as me but as time passed I had learned many lessons about my family. They were, in a sense, only on loan to me, given to me and Ivan as very special gifts from God to look after as best we could for Him, but really there was very little I could do to keep these little ones alive every day if God hadn't given them life. I'm not abdicating responsibility, I know very well that, as parents, we all play a huge part in the general well-being of our children and it's right and proper that we do. Nevertheless, at the end of every human effort, it is ultimately God who has given these little ones life and breath.

He had lovingly and gently spoken into my heart the understanding that a much greater hand than mine was in charge. Now I can see more clearly than ever before that life, all life, is God given and we cannot choose how long it will be, or how short. We cannot protect anyone from death by being the most protective parent in the whole world. It makes no difference, life is God's to give and take as He chooses. If we could control these things we would make such a mess of it. Life would never be long enough and most of our decisions would be made for us and not the other person. Yes, I had come a long way in relinquishing control over my life, but not by choice. It had been purely and directly the work of God in my life, leading me a road He had chosen for me from before the foundation of the world. Psalm 139

I was slowly learning these very important truths. You see, if you don't have Jesus in your life you don't have life anyway.

Life is completely useless and meaningless without Him. We need to fix our eyes on eternal things, not on how things are going in this life but rather where we will spend eternal life. THINK ... God has worked out this amazing plan to get us mere mortals back into a right standing before Him so that we can be totally acceptable to enter into his presence. He, the living God, sent His one and only son, Jesus, into this world as a man to live like you and me, identifying with us in our weaknesses and yet being able to overcome them in order to bridge the gap between us and God that was created by our sin. He had already worked it all out and He did it all for me and then gave it all to me, free of charge. All I now have to do to become a child of God is to believe it, accept its truth and acknowledge that I need Jesus in my life.

What freedom there is in this. It was God's plan and He did it all so that I could spend eternity with him in Heaven. For me then, eternity and Heaven had become a certainty based on these truths which were a living reality in my own life. Life without that knowledge of certain eternity must be so empty, pointless and without peace. Believing in all that Jesus had done for me, filled me inside, pointed me in a definite direction and caused me to have such a peace about the future that I just know I would not otherwise have had.

My conclusion then, was this, although looking at my natural condition, life seemed empty and pointless, inside me this wonderful new life of the living Lord Jesus rose up from deep within me, taking a much higher place in my mind and body than the condition I found myself in. It was not just positive thinking that we hear so much of these days, it was my mind being transformed by the indwelling life and power of the Holy Spirit which He gave to me as a free gift promised to me by the Lord Jesus when He rose from the dead. He said it was better for Him to leave this world and go to the Father so that He could send the Helper, the Holy Spirit, to live in each person who would receive Him, making it possible for every believer to have new life.

Born again Christians.....what are they? That's a good question. Some folks say it's just a new fangled American idea, but is it? What do you think? For me it doesn't really matter what any of us think about it, the Bible clearly says we must be born again. Jesus said it Himself while He was here on earth. John's gospel Chapter 3, Jesus has this conversation with a Jewish leader named Nicodemus. This was a man well educated in the scriptures and yet Jesus said to him that he didn't know the very important truth that he must be born again of the Spirit. It makes such sense to me, because we are born sinful and it's not our fault and there is no way out of this condition in our own strength, try as we may. That means that Jesus had to come and do it for us and make it possible for us to be born again. The whole plan was so incredibly wonderful and so simple for us to receive and believe. Jesus has made it so easy to believe and I do believe. It is a belief which will go with me into eternity until the day the Lord calls me home to be with him forever.

COUNTING THE COST TO GAIN THE MOST

Ivan had just arrived and we were settling in to enjoying each other. We had just been getting ready to go to sleep on the Sunday night, May 11th, 1991, when we heard the phone ringing. Fiona shouted up the stairs for me but Ivan went. He wasn't long away and I couldn't quite hear. Could it be....? Yes, this was it! A liver had become available........a perfect match for me! The Q.E. wanted me in first thing in the morning. We were really shocked as we had never really expected it to be this soon but it was great news. I felt excited, scared, nervous and everything mixed up together. This was the moment we had all been waiting for, but it seemed to come on us too soon and suddenly life took another quick dramatic change. I wondered how was I going to cope with this and knew that only time would tell. Again, there could be no running away because there was nowhere to run. With no other alternative I simply had to go through with it, but now it was here. It was no longer just something that was going to happen in the far distant future but right now, not in 16 years time as we had thought at the beginning of my illness, but in TWO days time. Our prayers had been answered again but could I really trust God to get me through this next phase? Well, who else could I trust?

Fiona took us in to the Q.E. the next morning and she was excited too. She had become so involved with my whole progress that she was now a part of all the proceedings. She dropped us off that morning just outside the hospital and she said she would be praying for me too, which I really appreciated. In

July 1990 before I became ill

March 1991 four sad kids

Rob, Fiona and Emma Dawson

33 Alpine Way

Me and Mum by the Canal

Sharon and me in the Q.E. - 10 days post op.

Vera   Carolyn   Jimmy   Jennifer   Helen   Rosalind   Moira
Mum (Jean)   and   Dad (Jim)

James   Lynn   Ivan   Moira   Jonathan   Sharon

the Liver Unit there were still some folks I recognised from previous visits. I settled in to one of the little side rooms first. I had always hated them, mostly because they were so lonely, and I didn't like being on my own with too much time to think about the next day. Monday was a long day with constant visits from doctors who took more and more blood samples, checking and double checking to get the perfect match. They must do so much detailed work behind the scenes that we never get to know about, but I was the kind of person who asked about everything so I maybe got to know more than most because I was nosy and I wanted to know exactly what was going on. After all, it was my life and my body, and I did have a right to know. Many thoughts were racing through my head because I had been reminded so often of the risks involved in this kind of surgery, such as the possibility of dying under anaesthetic or developing complications. Even if I did pull through, I might suffer rejection of the liver, etc.

By Monday evening, I began to feel a tremendous burden for my children, and in the light of all that had been said regarding the possibility of not recovering, I wanted to cover that area for my family by writing them all a personal farewell letter so that they all had something to remind them of me and my thoughts and feelings towards them and their future without me. It wasn't morbid, heavy stuff, just real heartfelt blessings for them. I began to write, wondering what could I say to this lovely family of mine. Ivan was having his own thoughts and he didn't think there was any need to write a last note as I called it, but I did. He felt sure I would be all right. I didn't know if this was an assurance he had from God or if it was just so much what he wanted for me and him. His attitude reminded me of Lynn's in the early stages of my illness when she was always reassuring me with words of her certainty that I would be all right. Deep down inside me, I wanted to believe this too, but the reality was that no one really knew, we could only hope. I was reminded of the text in Rom 8 v 24 *'For we were saved in this hope, but that hope that is seen is not hope; for why does one still hope for what he sees? but if we hope for what we do not see, then we eagerly wait for it with perseverance.'*

We were all eagerly waiting for this to be the cure, but we would have to wait and see and I felt it was only facing the issue to prepare for the worst and to expect the best. I didn't want to pass into eternity and not leave the thoughts of my heart with them as a reminder of all the good things we had enjoyed as a family. To leave nothing in the event of my dying, I felt would have been uncaring and confusing for them. As I began to write it was obvious that this exercise was as much for my own heart as for theirs. The tears started to flow and it was so very painful to face the fact that I might never see them all again in this life. I wondered again how they would manage, how Ivan would cope. "God, you have to be in this," I thought. "I have to trust you with their lives again as so many times before. I have to trust you with Ivan and my own life too. Help me to write words of life and hope to these dear special children that you've given to me."

I wrote to each child, beginning with Lynn. We had shared earlier about these things and she had talked about the plan she had to give up her course and go home to look after the rest of them. With her having a living faith of her own she felt it was an obvious choice, but I wanted her to know that it was not my wish that she should take on the heavy burden of a young family at the expense of losing her own chosen career, noble as the act may have been. I wanted her to carry on with her own life and not to feel responsible for the rest of the family. The oldest one in a family often feels this much more than the rest and I don't know whether we make our children like this or if it is just naturally there.

After a long time I completed the letters. I put them in my handbag and told Ivan where to find them if I died. I think he thought it was a piece of nonsense, however it was done and I had peace of mind now. I wanted them to know that I had no regrets and that I had one main wish for their lives, and it was that they, too, should find faith in Jesus and that they would not become hard towards the things of God because of what had happened to me. If they found this, they would have found the meaning to life and living, making it all fall into place and giving purpose and meaning to every area of their lives. I wrote lots of motherly sort of things too, mothers do, it's normal I think. God knew these feelings I had all too well, He was separated from His only Son and so here was another area of my life that God had experienced personally and more deeply than I ever would. I realised that every feeling I had known over this time of illness, He had known in a deeper and greater way. This comforted me so much and helped me to believe He understood me completely.

As I looked at Ivan that night, I wondered if I would ever waken up and see him again in this life. We talked over lots of things and Ivan prayed for me before he left that night. I was to have nothing to eat after 9pm that night, and all the time tomorrow was drawing nearer and nearer.

During the early stages in Birmingham I had met two nice Christian ladies who were part of a Prayer Chain Group and they said to let them know when my transplant was going to be and they would pray that day. The prayer chain functioned through sending a prayer request through the phone from one person to another. Apparently this group covered the length and breadth of Britain, so I was being well covered in prayer, plus everyone at home and others too.

I have read recently that investigation into the recovery of patients who have a faith and are prayed for has shown amazing results in the recovery of these patients.

I slept well that night, much better than I had expected to. The nurses asked me if I wanted a sleeping tablet but I refused. I had never felt it necessary before so I saw no point in having one now either. First thing in the morning, the doctor came to give me my pre-med, which is just a small dose of drugs before the big dose of anaesthetic. It was supposed to calm folks down before their operation. I didn't feel much different. Ivan arrived in time to wheel me off to the theatre. As we hurtled along the maze of corridors Ivan chatted and I felt good, quite at peace, although I now have no memory of entering the room where I received the anaesthetic. Ivan told me later that the nurses had commented on how they had never seen anyone so calm and peaceful before such a big operation. He understood why, but he never had courage to tell the nurse.

We had grown to know some of the people from the Riverside Christian Fellowship in Birmingham and they had very kindly sent someone round to the hospital to be with Ivan for the day, which was just the thing to do because it would have been a long, lonely day on his own. It was all very sudden for him to handle, as he had only come to spend a little holiday time with me and here he was witnessing the transplant day so soon, and on his own, which was not recommended by the doctors. They had emphasised how important it was for the relative of the patient to have someone to talk to and share with over the early stages because it's as hard for them as it is for the patient.

Ivan was very aware of how long and drawn out the day would be with nothing for him to do but think about me and what would be happening in the operating theatre. We felt that because a liver had become available so soon and had fitted in so well with Ivan's visit, the timing seemed perfect, but because it had been so quick we hadn't been able to arrange for any other family member to be down with Ivan. Sometimes it can go unnoticed how much the person close to you needs someone close to them for support, friendship and release from the tension caused by such a major event in their lives. Because of all this, we really appreciated the church fulfilling this need.

I had gone into the theatre at 7am, and for the first hour or so Ivan had gone back to Nuffield House for a sleep. He must have been fairly peaceful, too, or maybe it was exhaustion. He spent the rest of the time in the cafe or in the Liver Unit sitting room and the waiting room just outside the Intensive Care Unit where I would come right after my operation.

It was about 7.00 pm when Ivan first saw me. Dr. Mayer, one of the consultants who had worked on part of my op, told Ivan that everything had gone very smoothly and it seemed like the new liver was a perfect match. The operation had gone extremely well and so far so good. The next two days were pretty vague. I remember being wrapped in tin foil stuff and being aware of Ivan's presence. It felt so good to know he was there although I couldn't speak because of the breathing apparatus I had fixed down my wind pipe to help me breathe automatically. It was very uncomfortable and it seemed like I had tubes everywhere. The lights seemed so bright and they were on all the time and I never felt like I had any rest because every so often checks were being made on all the different body functions. If it wasn't that, it was a dose of some drug or another. A nurse was assigned to me personally to watch every detail of my progress, writing down and taking readings, carefully following her chart.

I don't really know how Ivan felt or how hard it must have been, just being there with me and not very able to do much. He was seeing all the tubes, etc., and feeling for me and all I was going through but felt unable to help. I want to say to any one going through this kind of thing, don't ever underestimate your value to the ill person at times like these. Words cannot express how comforting and reassuring it was to feel the touch and hear the voice of my loved ones as I went through this experience.

I had a terribly sore back between my shoulder blades, not a sharp pain, just a deep, heavy pain.   There were tubes everywhere. I had a couple in my neck, another line in my chest with several tubes leading to it and these tubes were for drugs to be administered through. I had two drains out of my abdomen and a bag for urine. I was fixed up to a machine to help me breathe, so in order to communicate I had to write. I did do this a little but my memory isn't very clear.

With the first day over, Lynn was to be arriving the next evening. I think Ivan was beginning to see the wisdom of someone close to share his feelings with. She arrived after an 8 hour train journey from Aberdeen and came straight to see me. She came right up to the I.T.U. with her luggage and we were so pleased to see her. We were both desperately needing love, and both pretty unable to give it, so Lynn was to us a little ray of sunshine that would brighten up the darkest day. She just has that way about her. Ivan was so glad to have her near because all the strain had been getting to him, and almost as soon as she arrived he vanished for ages, leaving her with me. Sometimes it is easier to cope when there isn't anyone too close to you. At those times, it's much easier to hide the real emotions, but as soon as you see someone close it has the effect of bringing them all out and we don't like that. I feel it is very important to let out all the feelings that build up or it just goes inward causing other problems. Ivan is a naturally quiet man, and it must have been hard to sit there on his own with me, knowing that I couldn't talk to him. Sitting with me, hour after hour, trying to communicate and me not able to give much response, was hard going.

Poor Lynn was thrown in at the deep end and I'm sure Ivan was glad to let her take over, but really it was too hard for her, too. I remember her loving touch particularly, it was just what I needed. It felt so good to be touched as she stroked my brow and my arms. Touching is such a lovely sense which God has given us to enjoy and I desperately needed it to aid my recovery, especially when I was so alienated from normality. It carried such a sense of love and feeling love which was essential to my healing. The touch of a loving hand brought healing to my whole being.

This was the start of me mending, and mending was what I needed. I was sporting a huge scar which ran down my middle from my breast bone to meet another one going from left to right across the bottom of my ribs. No wonder I had a sore back. I gradually began to pick up strength and my thinking began to clear. There were bleepers fixed to my fingers and toes reading my heartbeat. They kept going off and this was apparently bothering me. I wrote to Lynn, "I'm dying, I'm choking," and this naturally upset Lynn so she told the nurse. The nurse said this couldn't be because I was all wired up and if anything went wrong the buzzers would go off. I remember being annoyed by the nurse's reply and so I got the board and wrote to Lynn, "Does that nurse know what she's talking about, these bleepers keep going off." I was clearly still a little confused and the thing down my throat was really bothering me.

By now I was starting to sit up and I began to pull the thing out of my throat on my own. The nurse tried to stop me but it was too late. I was choking and I had half pulled it out so I suppose she had to pull it right out. The question now was whether I would be able to breathe on my own. The machine was to help me breathe but now I had to do it by myself. What a relief it was to get the thing out. I felt better already but as I lay back in the bed to rest I felt that my breathing was very faint, it seemed so slow and light that if I went to sleep I would completely stop. It was a weird and strange yet peaceful feeling, just like I was going to pass away. I told Lynn that I was scared to sleep because of this feeling but I did sleep and breathing for myself proved to be no problem.

Often, after a big operation, lungs can become infected and parts of the lungs can fill up with fluid, causing the lungs to collapse. I did not develop any of these complications, only one small area of one lung sounded slightly full. I was encouraged to cough it up but coughing frightened me. I felt that if I coughed too hard, I would split my wound or damage something inside. I felt tender all over and scared to put too much movement or effort into anything the nurses asked me to do.

I had been assigned a very pretty little nurse in the I.T.U., who had been sent by the nursing bank so she wasn't one of the regulars, but it was apparent she was well qualified and knew what she was doing although she looked a bit of a dolly bird. It's hard to think of a better expression for her, but she had all her wits about her. Every so many hours I needed drugs injected into all these different leads going into my veins and each one took a different dose, which was a complicated business.

I felt very thirsty and asked for a drink and was eventually allowed to have just a sip of water. That was probably the second day. The nurse told Lynn that I was one of the best patients she had ever had, which I took as quite a compliment. I think she felt a bit sorry for Lynn and tried to include her in some of the chores that needed doing. I remember her asking Lynn if she would like to help with washing me, which was a foolish suggestion, but I'm sure she was trying to be nice and include her. It was hard enough for Lynn to cope with all the tubes, pipes, needles, blood and yellow colour I had become, without doing some of the nursing as well. After all, I was her mum and it must have seemed so out of place for her to be helping to wash my hands and face. It was very, very hard to do, but the nurse said it was good to be touched in this way too by the folks that love you, because it also speeds recovery.

Lynn took a fainting turn and no wonder. It was all starting to be too much for her too, what a trauma for a young lass. I've tried since to gain some more information from her but it's still very vivid and painful for her and she cannot freely chat about that time, even though it's been almost 6 years since then. I do completely understand how she is feeling because when I read over the pages of my little notebook I can become overwhelmed with emotion myself at the memory of some of these times we all went through, but writing it all down has been a great release for many of these suppressed feelings for me.

It was now the second day after transplant and I was becoming very aware of others around me. Across the ward from me there was a little baby who had had a transplant Apparently, medical expertise is such now that they can cut down an adult liver to fit a child, providing all the necessary plumbing, as they call it, is there. What incredible skills these doctors have been given to preserve life. To the right of this little child was a very sad, ill looking lady who looked so gaunt and deathly, I didn't like it.

After a transplant, a blood clot can gather in one of the newly grafted veins, which can be serious, so in order to prevent this becoming a problem, they use a scanner. A smartly dressed English doctor scanned me with the ultra sound scanner and I marvelled at what a fantastic piece of equipment in modern medicine this is. I didn't like it at all, though, as he pressed so hard and I felt so tender still. Sometimes I wished these doctors knew what it felt like to be on the other side of their machines and prods and I'm sure they would have been much more considerate and gentle. Nevertheless, they had a job to do and they were good at it, which was fortunate for their patients.

All patients had to take a liquid medicine called Nystatin, to keep down the risk of developing ulcers and thrush in the mouth. If these took hold too soon after transplant, they could jeopardise health and hinder recovery. It was absolutely disgusting, a bright yellow substance which caused me to feel sick every time I took it. It would have been fine if I could have washed it down with a mouthful of water but that would have defeated the purpose of taking it in the first place. By now, I was being allowed a few more sips of water through a straw, ice cold and so, so lovely. I was making good progress with no set backs at all.

Lynn and Ivan each had a room in Nuffield House. Even though the rooms were fairly basic, they were a great provision for us. Lynn was always nervous in strange surroundings, a bit like myself, and because she and Ivan had so little time during the day to catch up with each other, Lynn would go into his room and talk away into the night. Finding any kind of security or sense of belonging at times like this is very hard. The strange places, unknown faces, nothing familiar, all reinforced the doctors' advice for the need for family members to be together. Imagine how very hard and exhausting it can be day in day out, trying to keep your spirits up as well as those of the patient. We were so thankful that Lynn had come and Ivan said how nice it was to have her to talk to after they went back at nights. At this time they were a comfort and strength to each other, a fantastic team. Ivan gave the quiet, confident strength and Lynn the tender, loving touch, what a blessing they were to me.

I had now discovered that the gaunt looking woman across from me had actually had a second transplant. No wonder she looked awful and she had other complications too, kidney failure, blood sugar level too high, extremely bad mouth ulcers. There was a look of death about her that really scared me.

It's amazing how we all react differently to trauma. I had always been a fearful sort of person and after transplant these fears were totally out of perspective. A lot of my thinking became irrational and I was pretty stressed most of the time which I realise now was just a normal shock reaction. If I compared my reactions to some other patients I wasn't really too bad. Not the best, but not the worst either, and I draw a little comfort from that.

I was moved into the High Dependency Unit adjoining the Liver Unit on the third day. This unit had a couple of highly skilled nurses delegated to look after each patient. The ward held 4 to 5 patients at any one time. I said goodbye to the I.T.U. and went hurtling along many corridors and into lifts again. I didn't feel that I was making rapid progress but the doctors and nurses seemed to think I was. Being moved meant progress.

The first day in the H.D.U., Fiona Dawson came to visit and couldn't get over how well I was. I could sit up now and was rather chirpy. I could enjoy a laugh and even crack a few jokes, but the back ache was still there all the time. That same day my local GP's wife from Orkney came in to visit me. She was down at a conference and I think that she, too, thought I was making a good recovery considering the extent of the surgery I had just come through.

By this time I had come to know some of the doctors and nurses very well and we could be a bit cheeky with each other. A French doctor who had taken part in the operation came in that day and in front of my visitors, said in his strong French accent,

"You will be pleased to know, Mrs. Scott, you are as beautiful on the inside as you are on the outside." Everyone had a good laugh and it was fair to assume he would have seen a lot of my inside. During these two days, most of the tubes and drains attached to me were removed and I was allowed to get up and sit at the side of my bed. I felt so weak across my middle, almost like I was going to fall apart, but also it was plain to be seen that my strength was growing every day now. I felt ready for some food too and kept asking if I could have something to eat, but they said I could only have liquid just yet. Eventually they gave in reluctantly, certain that I would be sick but I took everything they gave me and my appetite came back very quickly and I was never sick.

Ivan and Lynn had now moved out of Nuffield house and had been given hospitality at the home of Ian and Julie Greenwood, members of the Riverside Fellowship. Ivan really took to them and enjoyed Ian's company, a light relief from the usual drudgery of hospital routine I suspect. Lynn on the other hand felt the move strange and lonely being put up in an attic bedroom in yet another strange place for her. We were thankful for people like the Greenwoods, opening up their home to complete strangers, belonging to the family of God is very moving at times like these and friendships were kindled that have grown and lasted since that time. They have been in Orkney since and we have made several trips back there over the years.

WALKING FORWARD

As the fifth day arrived, I was ready to be moved again onto the main Liver Unit. This was an exciting and nerve racking moment for me. I still had something attached to me but I was ready to walk, Ivan on one side of me to steady me, and a nurse on the other. To me it was a huge achievement, not quite Olympic speed, but I was mobile again on the fifth day after my op. What an answer to prayer. I was a bit wobbly but my strength was growing quickly. Every new adventure seemed such a big step for me and it took everything in me just to step out and do it.

Meanwhile the physiotherapist was attending to me every day, giving me exercises and a breathing monitor to encourage me to take deep breaths to clear out my lungs. I didn't like it much because it hurt and the last thing I felt like doing was coughing. I had been warned that after operation, my resistance to bugs would be very low so when I got out I would have to be very careful to stay away from children's diseases, colds and any other bugs. I had always been a person who was very fussy about hygiene, so dirt and bugs were already something that bothered me. Cats and dogs were also to be avoided and definitely no close contact with them, this was not difficult as I had never been much of a lover of pets. They were bearable if they were somebody else's and stayed away from me. They were a nuisance around transplant patients mainly because they carried the risk of infections. My natural fear of bugs had developed into a phobia, probably because of being physically low and having had such major surgery. The shock and stress alone, strongly influenced my reactions and in some ways it was to be expected.

By now I walked to the toilet with help and how clearly I remember that first bath on the fifth day. It was such a lovely, soothing, relaxing feeling being lowered down into the water. The hospital had a wonderful contraption that I sat down on and they could mechanically lower me so it was very painless although all my movements were easier every day. I felt I could have stayed there for hours. The same lifting apparatus was used to fish me out so I just had to sit there and let the machine do the rest. Everyone remarked on how well I was looking, although my first peep into a mirror revealed how yellow I looked. Before the operation, I had been more a tanned brown colour, but now I was a bright yellow. It gave me a fright, even the whites of my eyes were yellow.

Every day lots of blood samples were taken by the experts who hardly ever missed the vein, unlike some of the young doctors who frequently missed. I hated it, it was so painful. These blood tests monitored progress and indicated any signs of rejection, something which was almost inevitable at some point in the early stages. One of the tests showed up mild rejection which they attempted to counteract with a huge dose of steroids over the course of a few days. I was aware that I might never come out of it and knew of others who hadn't, but this was just another hurdle to get over, and one among many others I faced during the next few weeks and months. When I went into rejection I needed to have a biopsy to read exactly how severe it was and then the doctors could prescribe an appropriate dose for me. I had a huge dose twice a day for three days.

My appearance up to now had not been great but after my dose of steroids I began to develop fuzzy facial hair and fat chubby cheeks, a bit like a gerbil. They got so fat I could feel them at the sides of my mouth when I ate. It was all a bit embarrassing but thankfully, in the Liver Unit I wasn't the only one who looked like this and the doctors reassured me that when I stopped taking the drugs I would soon return to normal. I really hoped so, I didn't fancy looking like that for the rest of my life. Although my appearance had never been the top priority, it still mattered to me and it was hard to believe I would ever look normal.

Some people had strange reactions to large doses of these drugs so they kept a close eye on our responses. One man went totally crazy, hitting and shouting at the nurses, it was completely out of character for him. I'm thankful I didn't carry on like that, my only reaction was that I developed a big appetite . It had been good already, but now it was unusually good. I had always been conscious of a healthy diet, eating lots of fish and meat which was good for body building and repair, and I needed lots of that, but because my capacity for food had been small for so many months before the operation, this sudden change gave my poor stomach such a fright that it was barely able to cope.

Martin and Sue Scott came up from Cobham, in Surrey, to visit us. Martin is Ivan's younger brother and he and his wife are part of the leadership team of Pioneer People. Lynn had gone back now, so it was good now for Ivan to have some company again. Martin and Sue had come up by car and they were able to take Ivan out for a meal and a drive. It was good to see them although I felt they were pretty stunned at the sight of me because the last time they had seen me I had been very well and healthy. We had a friendly, chatty time and I was to be having a biopsy the next day to see if the rejection was under control.

I absolutely loathed biopsies, they scared me so much. A biopsy means lying absolutely still on my back for six hours after they had injected local anaesthetic into the area just below my ribs and slightly to my side. When that takes affect, they insert a large, thicker needle quickly to draw out a little piece of liver.

Breathing is very important to a successful biopsy, as are the skills of the doctor. I was fixed up to an electronic blood pressure monitor during these hours, too, which was to detect any blood loss which might occur if they had happened to hit a blood vessel or vein by mistake. Although these events were very rare, they had been known to happen and I think it was that knowledge which frightened me. Sensing the tension, Martin and Sue prayed with us before they left. How special it was to have Ivan's family with us and we were so pleased that they had made the effort to come.

The blood tests this time revealed that my blood clotting levels were too low, so they needed to administer plasma before the biopsy. It was yellowish coloured fluid which had to be given through another drip. I desperately disliked the horrible long needles that they pushed into my veins. It was always so uncomfortable and restricting, but medically speaking it had revolutionised the whole area of injecting patients quickly and effectively. It was just another essential part of healing for me and I had no option but to go through with it .

Nevertheless, it was all getting to me now and I was pretty tense. Being nosy about everything that was going on, I always asked the details of every procedure and the reason why it was necessary. I liked to know and it made me feel better if I knew exactly what they were doing, even if I didn't like it.

I became shaky during this process and I panicked and asked the doctors if it was the rejection that was making me tremble. I was very troubled to be told it was most likely just tension, because I really didn't want to believe that tension could have such a noticeable physical symptom, but that it did.

WHAT ! DO YOU CALL THIS MEDICINE ?

I was fed up and feeling low and Ivan was too. Oh, for some heart warming encouragement or some light at the end of this long, long tunnel. It was checking back the tears time again for me. I felt as if I gave in to my feelings I didn't know where they would stop or if they ever would. It was important for me not to give in to them, but the waves of self pity and sheer helplessness swept over me in a way I hadn't known before. They were never spoken, just felt, and that was all I could handle just then.

Letters and cards arrived daily and they were like an oasis to me, frequently bringing good news from home and words of hope and inner peace to me in the challenge of these troubled and uncertain days. While I was lying on my back after the dreaded biopsy, I received a letter from the young nurse, Mary, who had accompanied me from Orkney to Aberdeen on my first emergency flight. Her card read

Let not your heart be troubled

Whenever I am troubled
and lost in deep despair
I bundle all my troubles up
and go to Him in prayer......
I tell Him I am heartsick
and lost and lonely too,
That my mind is deeply burdened
and I don't know what to do......
But I know He stilled the tempest
and calmed the angry sea
And I humbly ask if in His love
He'll do the same for me.....
And then I just keep quiet
and think only thoughts of peace ,
And if I abide in stillness
My restless murmuring cease .

Helen Steiner Rice

To dear Moira from Mary, take care and God bless.

Mary had taken the time to write a touching special letter, too, and as Ivan and I sat there in the hospital that day we both knew deep down in our hearts that these simple words of encouragement had reached deep into our innermost being, bringing hope, peace and comfort to our wounded worried souls. She wrote of how my letter to her that day in the Kirkwall hospital the day she had failed her exam, had been such a blessing and how it had given her courage to sit again and pass the next time. She said how she had taken my letter into the exam room with her and that she had been so touched by the fact that I had so much happening in my own life to bother about her, she thanked me so much and said she would never forget me. I lay there as Ivan read the letter with tears streaming down my cheeks and a trace on Ivan's too, we just knew this was the medicine I really needed.

Encouragement is such a powerful medicine. It lifted me, released my tension, turning it to tears, and brought hope for tomorrow. We saw God in this. The timing was so perfect and the words so right and young Mary was the messenger of mercy to our weary souls. God will bless Mary. He has plans for her life and she will one day be His too. I pray it will be very soon. If you have ever felt prompted to write or contact someone in hospital that you may hardly know, take the time to do it. You too might be to that person an angel of mercy bringing hope. These inner promptings are so often of great value to another person.

ON THE MOVE

When I had been on the move for a few days, it was suggested that we could go out for a walk or go over to visit Nuffield House where Ivan had a room. One wheelchair was much more streamlined than the others and was always in great demand by the patients. Ivan often took me out for walks in the chair, and one day, for the afternoon break when it was not a very nice day, we decided to go over to his room and rest there instead. It felt so good to be outside and feel the cool breeze on my face although it seemed colder than usual, as we were well into May. The bumps on these rides felt so big.

I had been at Nuffield many times before, but never since my transplant. My movements were slow and stiff and we parked the chair and walked along to his room. It was the first time we had been completely alone since my operation and it was so special to be alone in a private place at last. We had a decent hug, but not too hard and it felt so good. We lay on the bed together, relaxed in each other's company and relished a little bit of privacy just to talk and be ourselves. The wards were always so distracting and impersonal.

I wondered if I would ever be able to love Ivan normally again, and if I would ever be completely well to enjoy our lives together as a husband and wife with a normal family life. Inside I longed for that, but I was scared to let my heart get carried away believing it. I felt I had so little to give Ivan and I needed to receive so much love and care from him, he was so good to me and good for me, he never even once, not even for a minute, implied that I wasn't any good to him, he always made me feel I would be better, he always made me feel loved just the way I was. I never felt he was growing tired of me being ill and I always felt he was pleased to see me, no matter how I looked. The depth of love and commitment over this time was invaluable.

It's a sobering experience to realise you are the one with nothing to give the other person in a relationship, and yet the other person still comes towards you with a new deeper sense of love. We both fell asleep there in his room that day and it was the most relaxing uninterrupted sleep I had known for a long time. There's just something about hospitals that so stifles these natural responses to each other, the cuddles and kisses that we so much take for granted in our everyday lives. In hospital, there's always a lot of tension, plus many interruptions such as other people's bleepers going off and visitors coming to and fro, doctors, nurses, phones ringing, etc. How hard it must have been for Ivan, my quiet, shy man, and such a private person about feelings and emotion. He just couldn't easily relax in that kind of environment but his presence was invaluable to me.

We know now that God was teaching us both a whole new dimension to love and loving. I have always been a person who loved to give and show love in our relationship together, and I had often felt that what held us together was dependent on how much I was able to show him, but no. Now I was living through an experience which was the opposite of that. I felt too, during this time, that Ivan's display of undying love and commitment to me was revealing to me a much deeper truth of God's deep, undying, unconditional love for me which was not dependent on my display of affection for Him. It was not based on my performance and response, but expected nothing and gave everything.

This was a time where I doubted if things could ever be the same between Ivan and me. I wondered if I would ever be able to be a wife and function as a mother again, would I ever feel strong and well again? The fear and uncertainty was sometimes overwhelming for me and so, too, was this wonderful love that I was receiving.

As I looked at myself in the mirror in Ivan's little room that day, I wondered how he could love this yellow, whiskery, skinny, scarred and fearful woman. Yet I knew he did, and to be there alone that day, in the silence of his room with the closeness of his presence, was another great step in the healing process which made me want to be well so much. It helped me believe again that there could be life again beyond this painful experience.

No doubt, it was moulding us both in a very special way that nothing else could ever do, and was shaping us up into more whole and understanding people inside, able to identify in the future with others in similar circumstances. It also made us more adaptable to life's changes by forming character and perseverance in us as individuals, during these times when we were alone and on our own, having to cope without the other to depend on.

Walks along the corridors were getting longer and longer, Ivan always took my arm and off we set. Going up stairs was encouraged by the physiotherapist each day to get the heart pumping and to expand the breathing. I was improving daily now and feeling pretty bright and cheerful again, but I was not looking forward to Ivan going again in a few days time so I tried to shut it out of my mind. I pretended it wasn't bothering me very much, but in reality I had become extremely dependent on him and he was the best person for me over that time. He understood me, he cared for me like nobody else could and he was part of me, we ticked in time in so many ways. To let him go now, when I needed him so much more than any other time in our lives, was so hard, but I couldn't say it because he had to go. The family needed him, the farm needed him, and I tended to forget how hard it was for him to be torn in two directions because I couldn't see past how much harder it was for me. I had no choice, I had to stay. I was stuck and it was getting to me. I knew, too, that if I kept getting better as I was, I would soon be ready to get out for the first time and I didn't want to face that without Ivan, because I had become so dependent on him.

This was putting pressure on me too. Facing the outside world again, acting normally, being introduced to all the bugs and germs in everyday life was all a bit more than old Moira could cope with. However, unknown to me, I had developed a way of burying painful feelings and reacting on the outside as if things weren't getting to me so that on the surface it appeared that I was wonderfully accepting of things.

UNTYING THE KNOTS

The day Ivan was to leave, I developed a severe pain in my lower abdomen which was so sore that I couldn't move. He had to go because his passage was booked and Helen and Sharon were next to be arriving. I should have been getting out to Wolverhampton that day, but now with this terrible pain, it had been put off until they found the cause. Ivan went off to the airport to meet them and divert them to the hospital instead of Fiona's so they all arrived to see me and I'm sure that, for Sharon, it was a pretty shocking sight. I was so sore and due for a scan the next day. I had discovered that if I lay on my left side it eased a little. Sharon's first impression was not good. She gave me a hug and a kiss as I did likewise, but before I knew it, she, like Lynn, had taken a fainting turn. It didn't last long, but it spoke volumes to me about how she felt. Helen was her usual cheerful self and a wonderful companion for Sharon, it would clearly have been far too much for Sharon to handle on her own.

It was very difficult for me to adjust to them now, after Ivan. They didn't really know the score and it was difficult for them, too, but it had been a long time since I had seen them. Although they were aware of my condition, they hadn't had first hand experience since I had left Orkney, and really I had been through so much since then and was still a very ill person, albeit on the mend. They were totally unaware of how I was coping or feeling and how all these stressful events were knotting me up inside.

I went for the x-ray and scan and absolutely nothing had shown up on either. Ivan had now left, and parting with him had been so sad for me, so that now I could see that this pain was related to his leaving. I would never have believed an emotional pain could have had such a physical symptom had I not experienced it.

The thought of Ivan going had knotted me up so much inside that it had caused my bowel to go into cramp like spasms, causing me severe sharp pain. The pain gradually got less and less and I relaxed into Helen's and Sharon's company slowly. How complicated we humans can be. I had been in denial of my real feelings and on the outside it appeared that everything was OK, but in fact, the truth was that on the inside, it was becoming all too obvious that something was very wrong.

I'm glad I was able to work this out by myself without the doctors telling me, otherwise I don't think I would have truly believed their diagnosis. I'm glad, too, that I had the Lord Jesus living in me, because I'm certain being a Christian helped me to be able to look at myself and examine what was going on inside. I was able to admit that I had made myself knotted up.

Helen had brought me a lovely present, a new top with a lacey collar, it was welcome and I had just been wearing jogging suits for comfort, so to have something new to wear was special. The good thing about the Liver Unit was that we were made to get up every day and change into normal clothes and I felt that was right and it kept us feeling normal, instead of lying around the beds feeling like an invalid all the time. Whenever possible we were encouraged to go to the dining room for food, all with the intent of keeping routine as normal as possible.

Helen and Sharon were full of news about home. I hurt Helen's feelings one day mainly because I had become so wrapped up in my own feelings I hadn't thought of them and how difficult they were finding it to come down from their normal busy lives to be stuck here in hospital with nothing to do but sit at my bed side and talk. I had become relaxed with Ivan and he, with his quiet, gentle strength, knew where I was at. We would often just sit there in each other's company in silence and it was just reassuring to know he was there, and now these two companions for me were so different to settle down with. This day, I told Helen how hard I felt it, concentrating on all of what she was saying and how I felt it a strain talking all the time. I said I was sorry for hurting her feelings but I hadn't meant to, it was just that I had slowly begun to realise that the pain inside was not anything that the doctors could help me with, but that it was my own emotional inner pain and it would take time for me to work it out.

Strangely enough, after speaking it out to Helen and giving vent to my feelings and fears, I started to feel much better. I'm sure Helen didn't, she was trying her best to adjust too, but as the days went on I began to accept their help and we grew together too, and developed an understanding of how best to help each other. We had some laughs and Helen soon got into conversations with some of the other patients. Gradually the pain was going and the day of my discharge was imminent.

HUGS AND BUGS

On the tenth day after my op I was ready for out. Now I was feeling that I could maybe handle it, but I was still filled with lots of fears. Rob came to collect us from the hospital and what a nuisance we must have been for him. It was so out of the way to come and get us. The distance from Wolverhampton to the Q.E. was about a half-hour's drive with heavy traffic all the way. Because of my many trips over the months, I was beginning to pick out familiar landmarks. Rob and Fiona spent hours every week driving in these conditions, but for us, the constant smell of fumes was unbearably bad compared to a drive on an Orkney road. As far as the eye could see on a nice day, it was never very clear down here, not as we would know a clear day in Orkney. There was always a thick haze all across the West Midlands. Small wonder, I thought, since it was only a very minimal part of the road network we were on and with the West Midlands being so densely populated I couldn't hazard a guess at how many vehicles would be moving from place to place per day. Crazy, crazy people rushing around.

I have never been a person who felt comfortable in a busy city environment or on fast moving motorways like this. Give me the laid back, sparsely populated, wind swept island lifestyle any day, to this mad poisonous atmosphere. There was no point thinking too hard and long about it or drawing comparisons. I was glad to be here, I needed to be here. I was being tended to by the best and most skilled transplant team in the world, so the culture shock was a small sacrifice, after all. It was only a slight, momentary affliction, as the apostle Paul speaks about in Romans.

We arrived back at Alpine Way to cats, flowers, medicine, T Tube, etc. All these things took over for the first few days, with no nurses and doctors to depend on, and a list of things to do and not to do. I wondered how I would cope with all the medicine procedure and drugs. Fiona had two beautiful pedigree cats, Shan and Sharma, they were part of her family, but for me, now, they spelt, lived and breathed GERMS in capital letters.

It had been her birthday recently and she had received lots of lovely flowers. At the Liver Unit, flowers were not allowed on the ward because the water contained some bug that was supposed to be dangerous for the transplant patient. Instantly I saw the flowers, I began to panic. I just had to tell Fiona how I was feeling and she was so understanding about it. She threw some out and the good ones she removed from the living areas and put in her bedroom.

Looking back over that time, I am utterly ashamed of my behaviour to such seemingly trivial things, but that's how it was for me then. Suddenly all the little things seemed to panic me. This was the real me and I could only be me. I would have liked to have been strong and fearless, but I wasn't, so I just had to get on with being me. I was still Moira, war wounded, bruised and battered, stretched and pulled in various directions emotionally and physically, but the same person. I cannot say that all my personality was exactly the same, because it was changing too.

When going through such deep, deep times in every area of life, it can only be life changing and traumatic but, because of my faith in God, I still knew that everything I was going through now would one day bear fruit in my life. This would not just be for my benefit but for many other people as well. I trust that with the Lord's help that will always be true.

Families are such a blessing, and Helen's and Sharon's caring and love were vital at this point in time. How good to have real hugs and kisses and be able to give them now as well. This was proving to be a huge factor in my healing process. Seeing folks from home kept me believing there was still such a place, although so far removed from the reality of my life just now.

They were so confidence building, and put up with my paranoid behaviour about having to have every dish, spoon and utensil sterilised, but my confidence was also growing. One morning I felt so sure I would be able to swallow one of my tablets whole, which I had not been able to do for a long, long time. To my disgust, it stuck and brought on a major panic attack. Helen just prayed that I would relax and down it went, but I didn't try that again for a while.

At Fiona's it was much more normal for Sharon and I to have a heart to heart chat with each other. We often sat on my bed upstairs sharing and caring. I so missed these close family times, so every opportunity was treasured. We sometimes lay there listening to the personal stereo I had been given way back in the early stages and Sharon had one ear plug and I had the other.

Sharon had brought down a worship tape which Fraser Balfour had made for me and one song in particular seemed to touch me deep within. Even the tune seemed to be inspired by the Lord, and it came alive as Fraser played it. I asked Sharon if this tune had words and she knew them so she wrote them down and sang along with the tape. It wasn't something she found easy to do, being more shy about singing than Lynn or Jonathan, but she did it for me and as she sang, the words touched her heart, too.

> By your side I would stay
> In your arms I would lay
> Jesus, lover of my soul
> Nothing from you I withhold
> Lord, I love you
> And adore you
> What more can I say.
> You cause my love to grow stronger
> With every passing day.

These words completely identified where I was at and we sat there crying, moved by the special touch of God on our lives by the words of this simple beautiful song. Thanks, Fraser. Even yet, years after, this song can bring a tear to my eyes and it is so strange and wonderful how some things are so timely, just like a personal hug from above. In your arms I would lay.

Rob and Fiona were out at work all day and little Emma was at nursery, so we had their home to ourselves. Fiona had two ladies employed to come round and do the housework and I had come to know them quite well. They took a keen interest in my progress. They both had a very strong Birmingham accent which I loved to imitate, I expect they had a go at imitating me, too, out of ear shot. We tried to be out when these ladies came round, so that we would not be in the way. It seemed a strange concept to me having cleaners in, but then again I did too at the present time, only I wasn't there to enjoy it. In truth I would have given anything to be able to be home doing my own cleaning, bugs or not.

This whole new adventure had been pretty nerve racking for me, but was nevertheless a huge step forward on the road to recovery and normality. I had to decide to make myself confident and just do it and I could manage, but it wasn't easy. I'm sure that others, observing my behaviour over this time, were bewildered, and it's something I cannot make anyone understand who has not been there. I know now that I can really feel what other folks experience, and what they really need at times like these. You can't really identify unless you've been there yourself and if you have, it opens up your eyes to the inner pain and huge mountains and trials to overcome which most likely will seem trivial and insignificant nonsense to people who are well and healthy. Most of the time, all we really need is a warm reassuring hug, and to be loved and cared for into a place of being able to face tomorrow. After three days I was due back in at the Liver Unit for my first check up. I had done well and so we figured it would be a few blood tests and then out again.

WHAT IS THE TRUTH?

Helen and Sharon were not only a family support, but a spiritual strength too, as was everyone else who came. Every night, before leaving me, they would pray and this was a great comfort and my main life line. Life without God is no life anyhow, so in some senses for me, it would have been better to be dead but alive forever with Christ than alive but spiritually dead in this life here on earth. What a dynamic thing Christ has done for each person who believes in Him and accepts Him as their Saviour. How sad that so many people are alive in this world but have never had this wonderful spiritual birth which is the meaning and reason to all life and are consequently dead to the spiritual life Jesus can give to all who receive him.

Again, I asked myself why I should be so privileged to know this truth and reality in my life, knowing that I am not more acceptable to God than anyone else. The Bible says very clearly that Jesus does not want anyone to go to an eternal destiny without knowing Him. I'm no more acceptable, it's simply that when I heard the truth about Jesus preached, I realised that it applied to me and included me as it does everyone. Unfortunately, not everyone wants to hear or believe or respond.

No matter how hard I try to behave like a Christian, I cannot make myself spiritually alive. Believing that Jesus and God are real won't do it either, because it says in the Bible that the devil even believes in God and there is no way that he is a Christian.

What makes me spiritually alive today is the wonderful truth that when Jesus died on the cross, He not only died to take away the death penalty that I really deserved, He sent His Holy spirit to live in me. It sounds arrogant, doesn't it, to say I have God's Holy Spirit living in me, but it's not me who said it first.

Check the Bible for yourself, Romans 8 v 9. *' But you do not live as your human nature tells you; instead, you live as the spirit tells you to - if in fact, God's Spirit lives in you. Whoever does not have the Spirit of Christ does not belong to Him. But if Christ lives in you, the Spirit is life for you, because you have been put right with God, even though your bodies are going to die because of sin. If the Spirit of God who raised Jesus from death, lives in you, then He who raised Christ from death will also give life to your mortal bodies by the presence of His Spirit within you.'*

At Pentecost, after Jesus had ascended into Heaven to be with the Father forever, He said to His disciples *'See I will send you another helper to live in you even the Holy Spirit.'* He has made it so easy for ordinary human beings like you and me to understand and believe, but in many churches the whole truth is not explained clearly to us and we are often misled into thinking that being a Christian is based on our goodness or performance rather than the real truth. When we understand what is spoken of in the Bible about being born again from within, not trying to do things in our own strength but relying on God to place his Holy Spirit within us, when we see our need of Him to come and be the Helper that He has always wanted to be in each one of our lives, it is then that we are free.

Another lovely thing about becoming a Christian for me, was that God didn't take away my right to choose to follow Him and believe in His word. He could have controlled me and taken away my freedom to choose, but that was not His plan. He wanted people to be able to decide with our hearts and wills to follow Him, thus building a new relationship with God based on a new birth. I no longer need to try to please God or be good, with His Holy Spirit within me I will please Him and I will be good from a new desire within me to serve and follow, and it's not a difficult task but a great freedom and privilege to be a real child of God.

So I'm born again, converted, changed, made new from the inside. I no longer need to try to be good, I want to be good. I no longer just believe, but I am alive and renewed from inside just as God had always intended all mankind to be since Adam and Eve. I'm so glad someone told me this truth so that now I can have this inner confidence, not in me or in the doctors, not in vain wishful thinking or even a vague misty belief, but a real, living, active faith that my life was in the hands of my God whom I completely trusted and who knew me through and through from the inside out.

It was a stark contrast from the everyday, ordinary person with everyday, ordinary feelings, yet possessing within this deep spiritual life which kept me going, maintaining sanity and composure and giving me a purpose in all this and a sense of destiny that no doctor or family member could give.

We are body, soul and spirit, and this is what I saw being worked out in all these things that were happening to me. They all needed to work together to make the healing complete for my body, with all its damage and scarring, and for my soul with all the emotional trauma, pain and hurt. My soul is the part that makes me all that I am and my spirit is the part of me that was alive in Christ and it was all being tried and tested, stretched and challenged almost every day in some way.

I do hope that " me peedie thowts " are being clearly enough explained. I pray that God will give understanding to anyone reading this section to be able to grasp these simple truths for yourself and let them become a living vibrant spiritual rebirth for you too.

INS AND OUTS, UPS AND DOWNS

My return visit to the Q.E. was not as straight forward as I had expected it to be as the latest blood tests had showed up some abnormalities and a heaviness began to settle on me again. I wondered what could be next. Now I needed another biopsy and I hated biopsies. They meant lying completely still on my back for six hours with my blood pressure being checked every 15 minutes for the first 2 hours and then every 30 minutes for the next 2 hours. This was in case the biopsy caused any internal bleeding. It always freaked me out because, even though the chances were very slim, it wasn't a nice thought. The biopsy itself was done with a 2 inch needle full of local anesthetic which was inserted right in through the rib cage, just missing the diaphragm and through into the liver. Another, thicker needle was used to extract a small slither of the liver for the doctors to examine. I had to hold my breath while the big needle was inserted and pulled out very quickly and then breathe normally. They were suspecting rejection, which was another scary thought for me. Wondering if this new liver was going to be accepted by my body, I felt I just couldn't stand the thought of another transplant. This was a possibility and I had met and seen a few folks who had had two and the second one had been successful. I really, really didn't want to have another, the thought of it at the time was too much.

I talked to God about it and I told Him exactly how I was feeling, whether good or bad. I used to tell him I just couldn't cope with some of these events and the most amazing thing for me was that I didn't feel Him being hard and condemning with me, but instead, I felt the most incredible love and acceptance flowing out to me just as I was, where I was. I felt He told me He loved me no matter how I felt, and no matter how useless I felt my performance was in my own eyes and the eyes of others. Sometimes I would tell Him I just didn't feel like any kind of Christian witness, but only empty and very helpless to change things. It seemed to me that the Lord wanted me to speak out my weaknesses, faults and failings and then He would reach down to me where I was at, come underneath me and hold me there. It was such a release to me to discover that God isn't primarily interested in how we perform but in who we are. For me, He was more evident in my weakest moments than any emotional or spiritual high in my life before.

How great to have faith in that kind of God, one who reaches down with arms of love holding us and not us holding on to Him for grim death. Him coming to us in our need and not us striving to find Him, not us searching for peace but Him coming to us with His peace, touching our lives over and over again. These times were life changing, discovering over and over the new life surging up inside every time I gave my attitudes to Him and His life becoming a living reality as I reached out to touch Him in my deepest need. He took me deeper in these times of testing than any other thing could ever have accomplished. I am still overcome with many deep feelings as I ponder over that time just after my operation. Sometimes I used to feel that God had spread out His wings over my bed space and I would go to sleep at night knowing with such conviction that no harm was going to come near my tent, as it felt to me. I never actually saw an angel, but many times I felt the close presence of heaven or heavenly beings all around me. Yet, even with this knowledge, I still had to battle with fear and anxiety but through it all, Jesus came to me in them and just loved me there and said he would help me through them and He did.

When I first had these thoughts, I wondered if they were right thinking, and then some years later I had the joy of being present at a conference in London where a world famous Christian leader, John Wimber was speaking of his recent bout of cancer. Here was this renowned man of God, talking about the fear that gripped him before some of the treatments, but that God didn't condemn him.   He did not supernaturally remove the pain but He came down to where he was and held him there.   I cried tears of understanding because I could so identify with this man's story.   He knew, he had been there too, I understood that he knew the secret of going deeper with God in pain, loneliness, fear and yet being in the will of God.

It would have been much easier to have gone to be with the Lord, to be lifted right up out of it all, the messed up emotions, the weakness, the constant perseverance and never ending uncertainty, but that was not the will of God for me.   He had many, many things to teach me yet about all the ins and outs of who He was and what He could and would do through letting His life flow in and out through me.

MY CHUM , MY MUM

The biopsy showed that there were still signs of rejection there, so I had to take another huge dose of steroids to counteract it. Next on the list to visit was Jonathan and Mum, they were to travel together and I'm not quite sure who was looking after who, it was probably a little   bit of both really.   Jonathan, although just a young lad of 14, was well mature for that and very alert when it came to travel, perhaps more than his granny, but she added that necessary ingredient to the team called motherly common sense and tender loving care.   When I had asked the family who would be coming next and was told that Jonathan was very keen to come, I was a bit afraid because when

I had spoken to him it sounded to me like he had a dose of the cold and I didn't really want to see him unless he was healthy and well. He tried to reassure me that he was OK, but I was not totally convinced. Thankfully, he was not put off by my concern and just came anyway.

They were a good mix of personalities, and Jonathan was so young and full of fun and life, it cheered my heart to see him. He has such a good sense of humour, mostly developed by his uncanny observance of other's peculiarities, but because of his youthful light heartedness, it was received the way it was meant. Nothing ever seemed to bother him. They had come by jet and had been served a wonderful meal which he loved, in fact, any mention of food got him excited. He and his granny slept in the same room in old Nuffy Hoose, as we in the family called it, and they took good care of each other. The whole thing was so straight forward for Jonathan, who took me for walks in the wheelchair which I loved. I had become so hospitalised over these months that it was hard to think of life the way it used to be. We took it a day at a time and each day had enough of its own troubles to cope with without looking too far into the future.

I was improving every day and getting dressed myself, walking lots more, eating well and fairly good company I thought myself. I was keen to take an interest in other people's needs and had lots of contact with the many patients who were coming and going. Some of them stick in my mind vividly and I think I could write a separate book about such lovely people who were a real inspiration to me as their courage and zeal for life far exceeded mine. I watched them, as I have no doubt they did me, and each had their own story to tell.

I knew my body very well by now, and all the little ins and outs of the daily routine on the Liver Unit. At one end of the unit there was a sitting room for the patients and a dining area with a T.V. and a video recorder, which was a good place for socialising. We met folks coming in for assessments, check ups and blood tests, as well as the visitors who often spent some time there. It was a busy place and nice for a chat. I usually found that most people were like myself, ready to talk and share what was going on in their lives. We all need a listening ear when we feel alone and out of our normal pattern of life, and conversation flows so naturally with a complete stranger as we shared the things we had in common.

There were books and games in there, too and, one of my favourite games was Scrabble. Jonathan and Mum played faithfully with me and it was really great for keeping my mind occupied and alert. Crosswords also passed the time and my vocabulary increased, as did my skill with these crosswords and puzzles. Very, very boring for a healthy person I suppose, but a wholesome diversion for me. Jonathan wasn't bothered about my scar or colour or appearance but rather interested, in fact, he was very interested in the T. Tube.

This was a thin tube attached to my bile duct which needed to be flushed through with saline solution twice a day. It was extremely important to keep any contact with this tube sterile. I had to wear plastic gloves and everything had to be done to a strict procedure. It came out through my skin just above the ribs and had a little tap on the end where there was a small syringe full of saline to flush it. Not everyone who had a transplant got one of these tubes, it depended on which doctor did that part of the operation. I'm very glad now that I did, because it was to be a great benefit to me in the days that lay ahead.

Mum and Jonathan got on well for there being such an age difference, and granny was always full of praise for her young grandson. I was very proud of him, too, and such a delight to me when, every night before they left me, Jonathan, young though he was, said a prayer for me which took a lump to my throat. They took up residence in Nuffield house where most of the family had used the accommodation now and the same feeling was shared by them all. They hated the place, maybe it was the coldness, but there was just something about it. Nothing like home, it was a bit more like the college halls of residence in Aberdeen, in that it was very basic with sparsely furnished rooms, drab furniture and decor. The kitchen and bathrooms were shared, as was a communal sitting room. Maybe it was the atmosphere of the place, since all the people occupying it had ill relatives, causing a gloom and heaviness over the area. It was not surprising really that my family felt uncomfortable there, and the memories it held were frequently those of doubt, fear and loneliness, if not theirs, then someone else's. There was a cafeteria downstairs and relatives ate there at a reasonable cost, so all in all, it was an excellent location for the families so near the hospital.

While I recovered from the dose of steroids, I gradually felt more relaxed and confident, and during one of these scrabble evenings while mum and Jonathan were with me, a lady came to visit. She was Jill Pullinger, Jackie Pullinger's twin sister, hence the Jack and Jill, she said. Her sister Jackie had spent some time in Gairsay (a small island in Orkney) so the family in Gairsay knew about me and also had contact with Jackie and Jill. Because Jill lived in Birmingham, she had come to see me. She was such a warm understanding person and her life had turned out so differently to that of her sister's. She had just recently lost her husband, leaving her with a young family to raise and a large house in need of repair. I could tell that this woman knew the trials and burdens of this world because she had experienced them first hand. There was no pretence about her, she was so open and free to talk about her life. She brought me a book which was so appropriate, with little short stories of how some nuns saw the miraculous hand of God during the war in France. It was so easy to read and didn't need lots of concentration and it portrayed for me her sensitivity and perception of my situation. Even though she was a complete stranger, she was like an angel speaking the peace of God over me. If I hadn't been delayed with this second bout of rejection, I would never have met that lovely lady and missed the special place she had in my healing at that time. Another perfect timing encounter which proved to be a divine appointment.

I was soon allowed out again and my two companions went with me back to Fiona's, mum was very attentive now that she had me all to herself out of that wretched hospital. She is a typical mum, very attentive, who carried a constant worried look on her face even when she laughed, and no wonder, I know if it had been my daughter I would have been the same.

It was good to be out this time, feeling more confident and less fearful, I was slowly and steadily improving and mum was spoiling me with breakfast in bed and my wish was her command. Now we went for walks out along the canal again, not vigorously but comfortably, and most days we walked up to the shops. This was a wonderful achievement for me, but the cold was still getting into my bones. I had lost a lot of weight and so I felt the cold worse.

It was nice having Mum to fuss over me the only way a mum knows how. There is no one in the whole world that holds a place in my heart the same as my mum does, different from all the rest and I knew I held that special place in her heart that only a child can know. It's that deep bonding between mother and child which plain ordinary words cannot do justice to or find expression for, these deep things cherished and precious through time and eternity.

My mother, what can I say? Thank you seems too little and yet you never looked for thanks. You never counted the cost, your giving was always spontaneous from the heart, pouring out that inbuilt, instinctive, loving care that you lavished on me. I cannot repay and I know you never expected me to, but you set an example for my life, for my giving, for my loving, that has left an inheritance to pass on to my own children. It is that of a life laid down for the blessing of others, may I ever be a blessing to you, dear mother of mine.

It had been a joy to spend the days with those two, and as I looked at Jonathan, my young son, I was reminded again of how much I missed just being a mum. I'd been missing out on that for too long now and I longed to have them all around me again. Seeing him had stirred that natural instinct deep within me to give the kind of love that only a mum can, and I knew, too, that my precious family wanted that more than anything else as well. I wanted to be well. I wanted to be a mum again too.

SEEING ISN'T BELIEVING

Lynn came down by train from Aberdeen at the end of another busy term. The demands on her must have been a tremendous strain, however she managed her way through the year and got all the assignments in on time. It was about the middle of June now and the weather was pleasant, although I had expected it to be much warmer in England than it was. I usually wore a raincoat and it was rarely warm enough to go without one.

I thoroughly enjoyed Lynn's company and the days quickly passed. She was to be with me for a week and half way, though I was due in for another check up and allowed out the same day.

It was pretty tense over the next few days waiting for the results and hoping they would be normal this time. I was feeling fine and coming on well, but just as fate would have it, the phone rang with a message from the hospital saying that there was something wrong but they weren't sure what, so could I come in and get it sorted please.

This threw all our plans up in the air and I just couldn't believe it. I had been feeling so fine and walking longer and faster. I was doing more and more for myself and couldn't understand what on earth was wrong now. I was aware of a slight pain under my ribs which was sometimes quite sharp but I had put it down to normal tightness around my wound as it healed. However, off we set into hospital again, with Lynn a bit uncertain as to how she would handle this problem on her own. No wonder, it must have been quite an ordeal for her and especially the idea of staying in old Nuffy on her own. We just hoped it wouldn't happen.

The doctor explained that my blood levels were wrong, indicating a bile leak into my abdomen so I needed to have a scan to see what was what. Sure enough, the scan showed up a very slight leak where the bile duct had been joined up in the operation. This apparently was another very common complaint with liver transplant patients and usually curable, but for me it just spelled out another set back and a huge disappointment that I hadn't counted on.

I felt so sad and utterly helpless for Lynn, knowing she was hating every minute of this. I'm sure it would have been hard enough to cope with an ill mother at home, let alone here in strange surroundings and with no one to talk to, plus the prospect of spending the night in Nuffield House alone ....poor Lynn. I was helpless again and I had to put myself and Lynn in God's hands. I felt tears welling up, I had so much wanted it to be straightforward this time, but we both had to accept it and believe there was a way through.

There was no fast cure for this, so the doctors felt they should leave it for a while to see if it would grow together on its own. If that didn't work, a small operation would be necessary. I really didn't want an operation and literally couldn't stand the thought of it. Because of the leak, the doctors decided to divert the flow of bile out through the T Tube into a bag to keep it from leaking into my abdomen and poisoning my system.

One day, as I was ambling along the corridor just outside the Liver Unit, I met Dr. Mutimer, one of the Australian doctors attending to me. He was my hero and whatever he said carried tremendous weight with me, being the first doctor who had treated me on my arrival in Birmingham. I had grown to know and trust him over these months and his decisions and advice had always proved sound. He stopped to chat, as was his habit. He treated me like an ordinary person and was always sincere in his conversation , so I told him about the latest events and how fed up I was and how much I didn't want another operation. He just looked at me in such a reassuring way and said "Moira, it's so slight, it's nothing to worry about. I'm almost 99% sure it will heal up on its own and compared to what you've been through already, it's not even a blip in comparison." I so much needed to hear those words of encouragement. Although I couldn't see any immediate change, I instantly believed him as if it had already happened. I had such respect for this man's medical judgement.

On the ward round that evening, the doctors all strolled round each patient's bed passing comments and making decisions about their future treatment, etc., in their usually indiscreet manner, talking so loudly and letting everyone else in on your private progress or not, as the case was. One of them suggested I should perhaps drink my own bile so as to absorb its goodness back into my system with its natural ingredients, mainly because it contained important salts essential for my well being.

A symptom caused by this bile diversion meant frequent trips to the toilet (not pleasant, I recall, and the stomach cramps caused by the leak were pretty painful). I thought that Dr. Neuburger was joking about the bile but he wasn't and I was to be sent home again with this next unthinkable task looming, surely they could not be serious. To actually drink my own bile ...... YUK !

Lynn was not coping too well with the whole business. I used to walk back with her at nights along the tunnel that led to Nuffy. Attacks had taken place there before and I went for Lynn's protection, or so I thought. It's an incredible picture to imagine this pathetic, invalid woman ready to ward off any would be attacker, ridiculous, but we were a comfort to each other. I think my appearance would have been more effective than my strength and I certainly wasn't afraid of anyone attacking me. This place was now a sort of second home to me and it didn't give me the same scary feeling that it gave to the family, in fact, for me it was a place of security, and when complications arose I felt much better being in the Q.E. than anywhere else. Together we made it and we were soon ready for out again, heaving a sigh of relief.

The bile was to be taken in some sort of beer or ale, and never having been a drinker of alcohol anyhow, it seemed amazing to be prescribed it by the medical profession for a liver complaint, but I believed that they knew best and I did as they said. Every trial of the whole transplant saga had its own detestable element to it but was just tolerable, however this was the very worst thing so far in the actual doing of it. I cannot express how grotesque the taste of the stuff was, they must have been kidding, it was a joke, surely it was. It was like drinking your own spew, and the smell was vaguely disguised by the ale but not well enough. It certainly wasn't the sort of liquid you could sip and relish. It took every grain of will power I had to get the glass to my mouth. I would stand for ages trying to psyche myself up to swallow the stuff, and when I finally did it all had to go at one time with no breather in between. The consistency was a slimy greasy mess, and oh dear, as I write now I can still feel sick at the thought. Nevertheless, I was willing to put all the anguish aside, blindly believing this was right, this was good for me and I must do it because the doctor said so. I understood it was for my essential healing and contained the natural salts and fats needed for my recovery .

On my next visit to the Q.E., I expected a huge complimentary approval for being so diligent in carrying out this horrible task. Ivan, (who had replaced Lynn) and I, went together to the outpatients clinic this time and I saw one of the senior consultants, (better known as God by the staff). I didn't like him, he was a very austere man, aloof even, and although he smiled it was in a cold way which always made me feel that I was a mere weak experiment and not a feeling, vulnerable, convalescing person in need of understanding. This man's company made me feel that the top priority wasn't me, the person, but my statistics and charts. Thankfully, Ivan had come into the room with me and he heard all the conversation, so I didn't imagine it. This senior consultant asked me how I was and I proceeded to tell him about my achievement at the bile drinking. He just looked at me accusingly and said, "Who told you to do that? " so I explained the story to him. He asked how much I had taken and I proudly told him. Staring coldly at me, he said, "Well, I'm telling you now not to do that any more," along with other hurtful comments. Needless to say, this threw me into complete confusion as I believed I was doing what the doctor ordered and now, to be told the complete opposite was more than I could handle. It seemed that whatever I told him any other doctor said, he said the opposite.

I managed to control myself until I got out of there and then I began to panic. I began to cry and hung my head, unable to speak because of the utter shock. I couldn't take anything in, I just wanted to get out of that place. I wondered what I was to do now and who I could believe. A lovely young nurse, Ruth, who was a Christian I had met often on the Liver Unit, saw my plight and came over to my rescue. She comforted me and said to pay no attention to him as he was renowned for this kind of upset. She let us talk with Dr Mutimer before we left and he was able to bring a balance to the situation, speaking words of wisdom and understanding to my squashed ego. I found out through that conversation with Dr Mutimer that I could have been prescribed tablets that would have replaced all the goodness my body needed. That was surely a test I could have done well without.

WAITING FOR GOD

I had another return appointment for an x-ray to check the bile duct leak. Even though I was getting really fed up of these constant trips back and forth to the hospital, it was necessary, so I tolerated it. I was feeling very alone and it was so tiresome to sit in the waiting room for my turn in the queue. Sometimes it would take hours and by now I had spent endless hours waiting, staring at the walls with nothing to do. It was so boring and mindless, constantly looking at other people more ill than myself, each with their own worries and pains.

As I waited there that morning, I began to question God, putting Him to the test, you could say. Are You really here? I questioned. Do you really care for me? Are you really interested in how I'm feeling right now? I needed to know. Are you in this place? I want to see You, please show me in some way. These were my thoughts there in the waiting room and almost at once my eyes fixed on a woman sitting close to me reading a little booklet with C.W.R. initialled on it. I began to come alive, here was a Christian and I decided to ask her. She certainly was, and clearly was keen to talk. She was on the same wave length as me, very open and eager to share her faith and her church background with me. The time flew by and before I knew it, it was my turn for x-ray. This was a little chance meeting with a complete stranger and yet we had so much in common. It didn't matter that we didn't know each other or that we would likely never see each other ever again, I knew that God was showing me in this practical way that He was here with me and that He did care.

Ivan turned up just after my conversation with the lady and I was full of it. I told him about this instant answer to prayer which was God's perfect timing. Awaiting the news of the x-ray, I was resting on my bed and noticed opposite me a middle aged man lying on his bed. He'd had a transplant some weeks ago and his wife and family made constant diligent visits to the H.D.U. over these first weeks. They reminded me of my own young family, their boys were teenagers and the wife was young like too. She was very attentive of her husband and, although I had noticed them, we had never really spoken to each other apart from the occasional hello in the passing.

He had been in the outpatients that day I had been so upset and now his wife came across the ward over to my bed and said how much better I was looking. No wonder, if the last time they had

I explained to her my problem that day and she shared with me how her husband had had a similar experience with the same doctor which made me feel better. At least I knew now that I was not over reacting. She began to tell me about her husband's transplant operation, saying he had a very slim chance of survival and they thought he wouldn't make it but without it he had no chance at all. She said the church they belonged to in Birmingham had fasted and prayed for him and his recovery was just a miracle.

Well, this woman was a Christian, too. "Yes, God, You are in this place," I said. I couldn't stop smiling as I shared with her my story. We were mutually blessed and just as we finished talking she said, "Oh, by the way the woman in the bed next to you is a Christian, too." Wow, does God care? Was He in this place? Did He want me to know? Did He answer my cry? Yes, yes, yes, yes, yes, yes, most definitely Yes. I really never looked back after that, the bile duct healed on its own and it was just another little test in trust.

If I hadn't gone through all that suffering, I wouldn't have known the tremendous provision of those three people that day. I realised how much God wanted me to ask Him for my needs and tell Him how I felt and the answer was there even before I asked. How much God wants us to know He cares and that He had made that provision before we asked. I was getting the picture......just trust!

SPORTING MAD

We relaxed, watching Wimbledon every day as we were both tennis fans but could never justify hours of viewing at home. It was nice for Ivan to have a break as well and to rest in my company. We had all day every day of the week to ourselves, and Rob and Fiona were home at weekends.

Rob was a keen cricketer and he spent most weekends at the cricket club. Being Scottish, I was uneducated in the scoring system of the game and Rob tried to teach me, with great difficulty I fear. He was also very keen on golf and we often sat up late watching the Open Championships. I got to know the players and began to pick my favourites. Grand Prix racing was another sport Rob was interested in and I even got caught up in that, too. It's amazing the interests I developed when sheer inactivity prevented me from doing anything else. I must admit I enjoyed these sports, much to Ivan's surprise, as I had always been pretty indifferent to Grand Prix racing in particular, it was fun being able to talk intelligently on these sports. We walked every day and evening and I was gaining speed and going longer distances all the time.

Little Emma was growing quickly and her granny Dawson looked after her one day per week. One of these days, while I was waiting for a family member to come down, I went out with her. It was great, and she took me over to her home in Perton which was a few miles from Wolverhampton. Emma had a sleep while we had a cup of tea and a chat. Jean was a very active, retired lady who loved to go on outings and holidays through the year. She was a small, well dressed woman and I loved her friendly, fun loving, motherly ways.

She took me into the hospital for check ups and to the doctor's in Wolverhampton when I needed a prescription, and often she would take me over to Codsall which was a small town nearby where there was a craft shop that I could buy all the needle craft stuff I used for my cross stitch. For each of my bairns I did a different original design that I felt fitted them personally, a little wall hanging with their names on. The girls still have them hanging on their doors as a reminder of that time and they talk of how treasured they are.

Fiona, being kind hearted as she was, took good care of her mother-in-law also, and she kept in regular contact with all her family. It was obvious she had a listening ear to all their needs and was very caring towards them, too. It was no surprise that she was so big hearted to me because this was a part of her nature. People often see an only child as being indulged and inconsiderate but Fiona certainly didn't display any of that. They had a group of friends called the crowd and they often went on holidays together, usually abroad. They had a trip planned later in August to France on a boating adventure. They needed to get away as their everyday life was so hectic.

George and Muriel, Fiona's parents, were down from Glasgow at the same time as Ivan. George was a keen gardener and was looking forward to getting some work done in the garden. He and Rob got the garden sorted and shifted a lot of stuff and generally tidied up. The patio was cleared too, and was a lovely spot at the back of the house enclosed on each side by a tall wooden fence which separated the neighbours' gardens. The back wall featured a huge cliff which ran the full length of the street at the back of all the houses. It was overgrown by hanging branches and trees which gave good shelter and privacy. The whole setting and atmosphere of the place was so relaxing.

As I said before, Fiona was an only child and the apple of her father's eye, as well as a very successful businesswoman, capable wife and mother. She always looked good and dressed perfectly, her outfits were smart and tasteful. They were an extremely smart couple, Rob was as smart as Fiona, always neat and tidy whether at home or work, even in his gardening clothes, everything was done to perfection. I grew to love this couple and deeply respected them, they set me an example to be coveted and their generosity of heart enlarged mine as I found myself at the receiving end of their provision.

turn over→

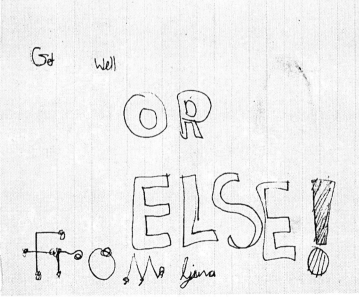

ples
mac
muera
betr
am en
e

Ples
ma s
mura
bettur

you wont be needing this again

AMBULANCE

From 5 years

HOME IS WHERE THE HEART IS

Where is your heart when you walk through unknown territory? Are you crying out for something familiar or can you step out confidently, walking forward and taking each thing that comes with a sense of challenge and triumph before experiencing the imminent victory? Mine definitely was a mixture of the whole lot as my emotions swung like a pendulum from one extreme to another, yet there was an incredible constant awareness of others, with their feelings and needs breaking in like waves through my own needs and changing stresses.

I had kept in contact with my home church and the constant stream of letters flowed in, giving fresh information of happenings at home mixed with encouragements and loving concern. The correspondence was filled with words of scripture to feed the soul and the mind, both of which have tremendous power to control the physical condition. I will be forever grateful for every word, thought, challenge and concern for me, for they brought life to my bones and strength to my inmost being. My hope in God never failed, my deep commitment was to Jesus as my ultimate Saviour whatever the outcome of this present darkness, and although I saw darkness, yet the light of the Lord was ever near and He consistently shone light and love to me as I continued to faithfully read my Bible.

My Bible was where my heart was. It was here that I drew the support I needed for inner strength, I soaked in its truth and many treasures were revealed to me in my illness with a freshness and depth that I had not previously known, enabling me to carry an invaluable ability to draw from resources beyond myself as I grasped some of the truths I read in the Psalms.

Psalm 118 v 17 : *'You shall not die but live and declare the glory of God'.*

Ps 16: *' You, Lord, are all I have and you will give me all I need. My future is in your hands. How wonderful are your gifts to me. How good they are. I praise the Lord because He guides me and at night my conscience guides me, so I am thankful and glad and I feel completely secure because you protect me from the power of death and the one you love, you will not abandon in the land the dead. You will show me the path that leads to life. Your presence fills me with joy and brings me pleasure forever.'*

Psalm 17 : *'Protect me as you would your very eyes. Hide me in the shadow of your wings. And when I awake your presence will fill me with joy.'*

Psalm 30 v 2 : *'I cried to you for help, o Lord my God, and you healed me You kept me from the grave I was on my way to the depth below but you restored my life.'*

Psalm 27 v 1: *'The Lord is my light and my salvation, whom shall, I fear ? The Lord is the strength of my life. of whom shall I be afraid.'*

Psalm 116 v 1 :' I love the Lord because He has heard my voice and my supplication. Because He has inclined His ear to me therefore I will call upon Him as long as I live.'

My home and my heart was to be wherever the Lord led me and for this particular time, it was here in England and never more true was the piece of scripture which says that we are aliens and strangers in a foreign land, and yet I felt an amazing inner calm about my being here as part of a much bigger picture that was somehow to be unfolded in the future.

The Bible clearly states that for the Christian, we are merely on a journey through this world, and that we are not to store up treasure here where moth and rust destroy but we are bound for an eternal destiny that will never perish or fade away. This thought leaves me with a feeling of how temporary everything here on earth is, and how wise these words from the Bible are and yet we need to create a balance while we are here in order to enjoy all the fullness of everything God has given us to look after and be part of.

My home was now wherever I most needed to be, and stuck here hundreds of miles away from Orkney, I was much more aware of the security and sense of belonging that often goes when we are in a way homeless and completely dependent on others for our everyday needs, acutely emphasising the concept that I mentioned earlier. We love to be in control and govern our own destiny, make our own plans and claim our own territory by putting down roots and making a false sense of being indestructible. How mistaken we can be, and sometimes we can say we know how fragile life is and also how little control we have over our own lives, but do we really understand how reliant we have become on so many of these driving forces that make their demands on our lives and have grown there deep within us, almost subconsciously dominating and making us believe we need them in order to be all we can be.

Life indeed is fragile and never more obvious than when we are ill and so many of us only cry out to God when we are desperate or there is nowhere else to go. Illness brings with it such uncertainty and it challenges us at every corner, making us face where we are really at. We have, up till then, concentrated all our energies and when we are deprived of our activities, we are, in a sense, forced to review our lives. We're cornered into examining what is of lasting value, asking ourselves where our heart is and what our homes really mean to us.

For me, my heart belonged to the Lord and therefore, through all this, I felt my heart had been kept safe, strongly affecting my whole being with a firm and resolute determination to cling on to the future, for me, for Ivan and the lovely children that we had been blessed with to look after and nurture and bring up in the instruction of the Lord.

Just before my transplant, I had started crying because I felt that I hadn't achieved very much for the Lord in my lifetime and now, here I was with the potential to be on the doorstep of Heaven meeting my Jesus, and I felt my hands were empty and I had nothing of great value to present to Him and this sorely vexed my heart. I prayed and prayed that He would speak to me and hear my cries and accept me with the little I had to offer, when suddenly I became aware of an overwhelming sense of His amazing love and acceptance of me. Into my mind, as if He was speaking personally to me, He said, "You know all the lovely children that I have given to you, remember how you have taught them of My ways and brought them up to love Me and serve Me? If that is all that you ever did in all your life, you have done it for me and have shaped their lives to pass on to their children. That is of indescribable value to Me, do not be fearful, I am pleased with you and your hands are full." The feeling of joy that filled my heart was incredible and the peace that flooded my soul was wonderful.

If you are a mum at home, sitting reading these words, don't ever underestimate the tremendous value your contribution and commitment to your children has to the Lord. I believe a mother has one of the highest callings placed on any human being, moulding and shaping a future generation. Time spent with your children is never wasted and is of eternal value, teaching them to pray, telling them stories from the Bible, singing little songs filled with the truth about Jesus, these times are precious and special. The home is where the family knows if your faith is real, they know if you practise what you preach. There is nothing more damaging to a young child than to discover that within their own home their parents are living a lie and that their Christianity is merely words and not actions.

Children can see right through any veneer or pretence so we need to know that we have the real thing and that our faith is personal, affecting every area of our lives so that they can grow up to know that faith is something worth having and that prayer and belief really does work. I believe that if we have a faith that works before their little watching eyes, they will soon develop a faith of their own and, in due course, produce a generation of faith children fulfilling the wonderful promise contained in the Bible of the blessings of obedience passing down through the generations.

If you are just reading this for a good story and can't be bothered with all this God stuff, that's fair enough, but I do still hope that you get some pleasure out of these pages. Maybe you have never considered any of these thoughts before and it's all a very new concept, this kind of faith. Maybe you have been a child of parents whose lives were hypocritical and strict, squeezing out the great love of the Lord and exaggerating the anger and disapproval of God at wrong doing and His shock and horror at our sinfulness, forcing you into a boringly regimental routine sort of Christianity. You have been robbed of the truth in being given to understand that you are not acceptable to Him because of how you do or do not behave or perform, but you are acceptable to him because of what He has done for you. He did it because He loves you so very, very much and He didn't want you to go through your life without knowing what He has done for you. He longs for you to find a real life changing faith too. Not a legalistic list of do's and don'ts, but an exciting life of 'I can and I will'.

Christianity is meant to be fun, it's meant to be wholesome, it's meant to be attractive and inviting and anyone who tells you anything else is seriously missing out on the real life Jesus came to tell us about. I can tell you for certain, since I gave my heart to Jesus I've never been bored and my life has never lacked excitement. Yes, some of the things that I've faced have not been fun, and if there had been any other way to go through them I would have chosen that, but Jesus asked the Father, too, before He faced the cross, if there was any other way He would prefer that, but not His will but rather the will of His Father in Heaven.

This time, I knew, was part of the Father's will for me and I would rather have had it an easier way but I know now that any other way would not have produced so many changes in me for the better. It was preparing me for many more difficult and deeply challenging things that I would have to face in the future. It was causing me to let my roots grow deeper into trusting the Lord, it was making me face the attitudes that were wrong, it was producing character and showing me more clearly how much Jesus loved me for who I was and not for what I could do for Him. He was showing me that He loved me if I never ever was able to do anything for Him ever again. How can I say this? Because it's true and because He made me, He formed me and knit me together in my mother's womb ....He designed me........gave me life ....He saw me before I was born ....so great is His knowledge and love of me that there is nowhere in the whole of creation that I can ever be out of His presence. Psalm 139

In conclusion, the home and the heart can never be separated. They are so intimately tied up together, entwined in feelings and emotions, people and places, familiar and secure things where we find an expression for our own identity marked on everything that we would call our own. God has given us heart and home while we live here on this earth and so it's good to know that on all these things and people we can imprint the mark of the Lord Jesus wherever we go. Others, entering into our homes and families, can feel the peace and sense an atmosphere without us saying a thing.

VISITS AND VACATIONS

It was now four and a half months since I came to Birmingham and home had become distant and unfamiliar, but this was the summer holiday time so I was expecting a few visitors. Family friends and church members, Sandra and Keith Corsie, were enjoying a short break in England and they came to visit. Sandra was particularly encouraging about my appearance, expressing that I looked better than she had expected me to. By now, with all the quantity of steroids I had taken to combat the rejection, I had grown a soft fluffy whisker and Sandra was so lovely, reassuring me that in a few weeks they would totally disappear on their own. I found that hard to believe, yet that is exactly what happened. Their visit was short but very welcome, cheering the heart.

My older sister Jennifer and her husband, Jimmy, were next to come. Jimmy's father had come from Wales to live in Orkney, so he and Jennifer were going to Wales for a holiday. They arrived by plane in Birmingham and went by train to Wolverhampton, after which they hired a car for the rest of their journey. Theirs, too, was a very short visit, but it was so good to see them and they paid a return visit, as well, bringing me a beautiful love spoon from Wales which I still treasure because of the memory of that time. I even came across the paper bag it had been wrapped in recently. Jennifer, with her quick wit and hilarious sense of humour, was always good for a laugh and lightened most conversations. We had a lot of fun which was just what I had been needing. Rob and Fiona's home was taken over yet again by the clan, but they seemed to like meeting all these different people week by week and that was just as well, otherwise we would have been lost for somewhere to go. I so much appreciated sharing the comfort of their home with my friends and family.

Another couple from the church were down south at the British Grand Prix with their family, so they, too, made a visit to the Midlands. Alma was a close friend of mine who had been a faithful letter writer during my time down south, cheering me with her news. I must say the letters were written on the oddest pieces of paper, often the back of some used school work sheets, but Alma has always been good at recycling and making things last, which may be Fraser's influence. Regardless of the reason, it doesn't matter because she was excellent at keeping in touch. Fraser was the person who had recorded some worship songs and hymns on a tape specially for me and sent them at a time when I really needed them. One tune in particular had touched my heart and this couple were very special to me. We had shared many good times together over the years, so a visit from them was extremely welcome. They had nowhere to stay so Ivan and I went B & B hunting and managed to get a place nearby.

My brother Jimmy and his wife Alison, Jacqueline and Fraser had not been down yet and they were to be coming at the same time as Mum and Dad. Dad hadn't been for ages either, so this was going to be an overdose of friends and family. On the first day that they all arrived we made a huge salad spread to feed us all, along with some mince and tatties. Fiona's lovely house was overrun with Orcadians so perhaps it was as well that she was out working all day or she might have found it much harder to cope.

This was more than a feast of food but also a feast of family, maybe just the right time to give me the big boost that I was needing to lift my hopes of being home soon. The next day Jacqueline, my niece, had a birthday, so we all went up to the Inn and had a sort of birthday party for her. The waiter catered for the needs of the kids so well, entertaining them and doing all sorts of tricks to pass the time until the food was ready. That night we went back to Fiona's and had an Orcadian night. Jimmy had brought down his guitar and we sang and sang all the oldies that came to mind. I felt myself spontaneously joining in. This felt good, yes, this felt really good, no doubt about it. It proved to be another major turning point in my recovery. What a treat! What a feast from home and they were all so encouraging about the way I looked. Like Sandra, they'd all expected I would look much more poorly than I did.

There were lots of hugs and kisses, lots of laughs, lots of news and just to be able to talk to them all was such a blessing. How very, very important to me their visit was, better than any medicine. How healing to be near close friends, how comfortable and non threatening I felt in their company. I'm sure they had no idea how much it meant to me to have all these people arranging their holiday plans around me.

Fiona and Rob coped so well with the invasion. Fiona had known Jimmy when he was a young lad, so they had a bit of fun talking of old times. There may have been a tear in her eyes, too, at the emotion of this whole visit, especially when they sang that old favourite, The Islands of Orkney. Any Orcadian will know that it can bring a tear to the hardest heart even when you live there, let alone being cut off, like I was. The singing of that song acutely pierced my heart with thoughts and feelings and strong memories of my old island home, and the flow of Orcadian blood running through my veins exaggerated the loneliness of the alien environment I now found myself in.

The kids, Jacqueline and Fraser and Kirsty and Robbie, had food on the patio out the back and at night when darkness fell they had great fun stirring up the bats. They were a novelty to an Orcadian and they would fly out of the trees above the cliff at the back of the house. Great fun and just a touch scary for them although I never actually saw these peedie beasties myself. The farewells were hard to take, but had to happen. Even though it was sad I felt I had taken a huge step forward, knowing deep down inside, that the next time I saw them would be back in our old island home.

FREEDOM FIGHTER OR WHAT?

All the time my progress was being very closely monitored, I had a drugs card chart where it had to be ticked every time a dose was changed.

The drugs were being cut down gradually and I was feeling better and better all the time. My appetite and strength were growing, as was my confidence, my walking was stronger and faster and I was able to travel further and further each time we went for walks. By now I was able to attend to the washing, hanging out etc. I had always been able to do my own but I had been pretty useless around the house for Fiona so it was good to feel slightly useful. I was very conscious, too, how little help I had been with Emma. With her being so young and needing a lot of lifting I just hadn't been physically fit to handle her at all. I could talk and play with her a little and she seemed to take to me, but all I could do was fairly limited. Emma was her own person and for being such a small child she had a strong will and was very demanding. She was fun and had a glint of mischief in her eyes but ever so cute with it. She was a special child and a little treasure.

My wound was still very tender and I only felt comfortable lying on my back. If I lay on my side I felt like I would fall apart, and I had a strangely hollow feeling inside. Nevertheless, I was slowly healing and I actually had a very clean, well knitted together scar which many of the doctors and nurses commented on. This was not surprising, because some of the patients' wounds were not a pretty sight and so even in this way I felt pretty special. I still had to call back to the outpatients for check ups and the last time I had been was when Fraser and Alma were down. The T. Tube was still attached and I was longing to have that last outward reminder, (apart from the scar), removed.

They drove me in to the Q.E. and I needed to go up to the Liver unit for more blood samples. Alma and Kirsty came up with me and it was such a good feeling to be able to walk out of that place without being admitted once again with some complication. It felt better than good, it was as though a weight was lifted off me when I realised that I could walk out on the same day I had walked in. Alma said I was like a different person on my way out compared to going in and could see the tension being released as I left. I hadn't realised how tense these visits to the Q.E had made me, but it was true, the feeling of freedom at being able to walk out of there was amazing.

It seemed now that the fight was almost over, the blood tests were getting better and better and all the levels were improving and I could see the look of triumph on the doctors' faces as they told me the positive results.

The fight for freedom and health had taken a radical turn, and freedom far outweighed the fighting now. I still had many fears and anxieties to overcome though, and they were going to take much longer to heal than the physical realm had.

STAYING IN THE RIGHT LANE

What is the driving force in your life? What motivates you and takes a place of priority over everything else you do? It's good to take stock and look at our lives and evaluate what we do and why we do it, because it may just be that you need to make a fresh start and consider afresh if you are in the right lane.

Maybe you are a canny sort of person who moves pretty slowly in the inside lane, taking care not to get in anybody's way and living life at a comfortable pace where nothing unexpected ever happens. If by some strange coincidence, something does happen, there is still plenty of time to change direction and take control of your own destiny ....or can you?

It could be that you are moving well in the middle lane, overtaking others with your destiny clear ahead, quickly advancing, covering ground and taking the opportunities that come your way. You have a sense of urgency to complete everything so that you can get on to the next challenging project and yet you still feel confident about your ability to pull up sharp if anything unforeseen crosses your path.

Maybe you are rushing along in the fast lane in life, with no time to stop for anything and no time or interest in observing what is going on around you, but being totally absorbed in where you are going and ignoring everyone else, leaving them far behind with a sense of pity at their performance and seeming lack of drive to get on in life. Motivation, speed and accuracy, total commitment to succeed, taking risks at every turn gives you such a buzz that you almost feel you are never going to fail or fall into any trouble. The faster you go the better it feels.

Perhaps you are not like any of these types of people, but we are all motivated in different ways. To appreciate the point I'm making, it's important to see that however you choose to run your life and whatever you do that makes you feel in control of the events that arise at the end of the day, are you really in the driving seat or are you carried along by an unexplainable chain of events?

That is just how I felt at the start of all this. I felt that I was in the driving seat of my life and that I had control of the things that happened around me and my family, so it's not surprising that when sudden illness came crashing into my life, it was so hard to break out beyond where I was. When this major illness arose, it demanded my immediate attention, forcing and dictating to me what the next move was to be, taking away my choice and making me submit to whatever direction circumstances demanded. It came as such a shock to me to realise that I wasn't in the driving seat of my life at all but was being carried along on a tidal wave of events which sent me crashing against the rocks. It was as though I'd been washed up on the shore and was lying there wondering where and when and how and why it had all begun and what possible purpose it could have. No matter how much I wanted to be somewhere else or somebody else or doing something different, I had absolutely no choice but to accept all the changes that assailed my life.

The secret life saver for me was to deal with the negative attitudes that various traumas caused to rise up in me. In doing that, I found an amazing ability to cope, overcoming my feelings to take control of them rather than trying to control events. When I did this, I felt my whole inner being relax and somehow it turned potentially negative experiences into learning processes about myself and how I functioned. I began to realise how I caused myself unnecessary grief.

Was it really necessary for me to go through such an intense time of soul searching scrutiny? Now, seven years on, I believe that this time has undoubtedly been the most refining and valuable experience of my life, and I would not be the same person had I not gone through it. I began to realise that to embrace the bad times as I would the good, is of incredible worth. As the apostle Paul said, "I have found in whatever circumstances to be content," and we don't really know that until we are tested in this area. Why are we tested ? The Bible tells us that we are tested to see if our faith is genuine.

'Be glad about this, even though it may now be necessary for you to be sad for a while because of the many kinds of trials you suffer. Their purpose is to prove

that your faith is genuine. Even gold, which can be destroyed, is tested by fire; and so your faith, which is more precious than gold, must also be tested so that it may endure. Then you will receive praise and glory and honour on the Day when Christ Jesus is revealed '
1Peter Chapter 1 v 6&7

Our lives are very much a journey filled with good and bad events. Our faith is a very personal and strengthening, and clearly a very precious, thing to our Father in Heaven.

Without doubt He is in the driving seats of our lives whether we recognise this or not right now, one day we will be confronted with this question. Are you really in control of your life?

When you face sudden, alarming situations in your life, how do you cope? Are you absolutely sure that you are in the driving seat of your life? ....THINK AGAIN!

The following is a prayer that can be very helpful.

LORD HELP ME TO CHANGE THE THINGS I CAN, WHEREVER I CAN, AND HELP ME TO ACCEPT THE THINGS I CANNOT CHANGE AND THE GRACE TO KNOW THE DIFFERENCE.

GONE FISHING

We were now well into the summer and the weather was hot, the season took on a colourful display in the beautiful blossom on the trees and the gardens were tended to perfection. I was delighted to know that James and Rosalind and their two boys Kevin and Andrew were coming down by car and with the weather so fine it would be great for the boys to have fun by the canal. I walked down by the canal every day; there was always plenty of activity down there, long boats and cruising boats, I loved to watch them going up and down through the locks. I used to spot birds there which I'd never seen before and little animals, like weasels, that we don't see in Orkney.

Nature is extremely invigorating and exciting to me and it was so refreshing to be out among it all. The variety of fish in the canal was amazing and types I'd never seen before either. I thought of James at times like that. How he would have enjoyed being here catching fish, compared to the long cold spells he would spend at the Harray Loch home in Orkney without much reward at the end of the day. I used to go fishing with him sometimes and as I contemplated the memory my thoughts floated back to these times so vividly. I missed James's little smiles and out door ways, here he would definitely catch something, albeit tiny. I had a sudden burst of inspiration as in my mind's eye I dreamed these things, and decided to buy some small fishing nets from the shop for the boys, feeling sure they would enjoy it too.

Just up past the canal and across the main road, there were

shops which I went up to almost every day, mainly to get out of the house and because it was a fine distance for me to walk. I bought food and snack things for the folks who were down with me, often I found little things I could send home to the kids. This was more for me than for them because I missed them so much and I felt I could do so little for them and needed desperately for them to know that I was thinking of them. It was my way of showing them I loved them and also I knew how nice it was to get letters from them, so I figured that they would get the same pleasure from receiving some, too. I made regular trips to the Inn for lunch, it was a lovely olde worldy place with rafters and lots of old fashioned stuff in ,which created a country atmosphere. It was like an old barn with ladders, sacks, buckets and dishes. Pubs in England are much more family places than they are in Scotland, where they are very boozy and not the sort of places you would like to take your children to, but here they were such social places and so friendly that I felt very comfortable being there.

James and Rosalind arrived on a lovely hot English summer day and it was such a delight to see them. They had their own car which gave us more freedom to go where and when we wanted. James was not accustomed to the rush of traffic but he did really well and I felt very safe on the road with them. Rosalind could have done with some of my confidence. One day we decided to go a drive to the Welsh border. I was really excited to be going because I hadn't been on a pleasure trip since the time Rob and Fiona had taken me with mum and Cally over to Ironbridge at the beginning of my time in Wolverhampton.

We set off in the afternoon and stopped often to give the boys a leg stretch. The countryside was very scenic and therapeutic until we drove past a farm where they had been spreading slurry (possibly pig dung). It was bad, I felt scared to breathe too deeply in case I took too many bugs into my lungs and throat. I never told them that it scared me because I felt they would laugh and think me silly, (which I was) but at the time it was very real and a huge obstacle for me to face, however I managed not to make it too obvious and it didn't dominate the whole journey.

It was the best day I had spent of feeling normal since my op. Being in a family, sitting in the front of their car gave me a great boost of confidence that life was getting more normal all the time, but the steps were so small along the way that I hadn't truly appreciated at the time just how far I had come. Before I had been diagnosed I found it difficult to stay awake on a short run into Kirkwall, the local town, but now here I was on a four hour drive and fully alert all the way. It was a day I remember with immense clarity and the sunset coming home was as red as the poppies that filled the fields and country lanes, highlighting the wonderful sense of breathtaking beauty, the reds and golds and greens and yellows making such a display of colour as the sun, sky and land finally blended together into a stunning red glow to end a perfect day. Life felt good and my thoughts wandered to the longing to see again the amazing sunsets I loved as I stood at my kitchen window in Howe and the words of the song The Islands of Orkney

The sun sinking slowly away in the west
The skies ever changing as day goes to rest
My memories will linger where ere I may roam
To the islands of Orkney, my old island home.

Was it just being away that made me feel that nothing could compare to the beauty of my lovely island? Whatever it was, my need to get home was intense and I tried to suppress it somehow, yet as I pondered home, its appeal grew stronger and stronger and my desire to be there again brought many a lump to my throat during that time of exile. My home, my Orkney, my roots, my family, my heart pounded with pride. I loved being an Orcadian, I loved my home, I loved my heritage and family and I wanted to be there more than anything else. Maybe soon.

James had a liking for freshly picked strawberries and so we went strawberry picking which was such a novelty for the boys. It was a lovely walk to the field through the English countryside and I was surprised by how many people were picking. When we got home we tucked in to freshly picked strawberries and cream. Yummy. Fishing was fun too, and we spent ages beside the canals which was a whole new concept for young Orcadian boys. I asked others sitting by the side of the canal the names of all these little fish to educate the boys and myself. We released them back into the canal when we went home but we'd had brilliant fun together.

The evenings were full of fun too because the boys took great amusement out of little Emma, and I poked fun at James and

Rosalind about how the boys needed a little sister to keep them happy. They really did enjoy playing with her and after she went to bed they used to go out to the back garden to stir up some batty activity, there were so many new experiences for them to take in.

Sleeping arrangements changed again and I had Kevin in my room occupying a camp bed. Kevin was older than my James, probably about ten then. Bedtime was a good time to talk; we would yarn and remind ourselves of all that we had done that day and sometimes we talked about what had happened to me, we talked about Jesus and ended up praying before we went to sleep. As I look back at that time it must have been strange for a young boy to cope so well sharing his room with an ill woman. I often wonder what he felt, he wasn't obviously scared and he was super company. It built up something special that will be there in our memories forever.

NEIGHBOURS - EVERYBODY NEEDS GOOD NEIGHBOURS

After James and Rosalind left I had a day completely on my own. This was the first time that I had been completely alone with absolutely no one looking after me but I felt able to handle it now. Olga, a friend of the family who also went to the same church as us, was coming down after she had spent a week or so in Scotland with her husband. He would travel back to Orkney and she was to come down by train. The family I had been living with were off now on a boating trip with their friends to France for two weeks so it was special that Olga felt she would like to come to be with me.

Fiona's neighbours were so friendly and caring towards me and I was touched by their concern, so it wasn't surprising that on the day I had expected to be on my own that they invited me round to join in a family get together they were having. I loved to be around Liz . She, too, had four of a family and had such a motherly way with her. They had rearranged all the furniture to accommodate the family and Baldrick the dog was kept well under control (which wasn't easy to do). He had a horrible habit of jumping up on people when they arrived. It was just his way of greeting, but it was scary considering the size of my wound. The party was just like I would have had at home and I felt so welcome, however, I hadn't been too accustomed to being entertained for several months and being in someone else's house eating their food was so very difficult for me as I hadn't yet fully overcome the fear of bugs. I picked and ate a little.

At home time I had been all prepared to spend the night alone, just me and the cats, but John, Liz's son, offered to come round and sleep in the house to keep me company. It would have been too rude of me to refuse and anyhow, I didn't want to. John reminded me of my Jonathan and I liked him a lot; it was so kind of him to bother. He was the one who often popped into Fiona's for a chat and to catch up with how I was doing, which I felt was very thoughtful for a young teenager.

The next day Olga arrived and we got on like a house on fire. We laughed at the same sort of things and had good fellowship together; we had the house to ourselves but the cats didn't like it very much sometimes. One night in particular they took a very funny turn and started jumping at the doors to open them and running around going under the beds and wouldn't come out and then when we finally got them out and thought we had them settled for the night the whole crazy carry on started all over again. I was a bit scared because I had never seen cats behaving like this before but Olga seemed to take it all in her stride. We had no idea what started it and it was the only time over my stay there that I had seen the like. Maybe they were missing Rob and Fiona, but it was really weird. Eventually they settled down for the night and we had no problems after that with the cats.

During Olga's visit, another friend of the family who lived in Edinburgh asked if she could come and spend a few days with me, and although I was well supported by Olga, we felt it would be fine for her to come too. She was Christina Mason, who was a first cousin of my dad and an older lady compared to Olga and me. We all enjoyed each other's company, lunch in the conservatory and sitting out in the hot sunshine, passing the time of day talking and catching up on all the things we had missed. Christina threw in the occasional old Orkney word to keep us from becoming too English, as if we ever would or could. Olga's visit overlapped Ivan's arrival, so he was able to help her with her luggage and take her to the airport.

OVER AND OUT

Ivan and the boys were down now and this was to be the last episode in this section of the proceedings. It was so refreshing to see my young sons again, especially as they were looking so healthy and well. I hadn't seen James since before my transplant and it was such a delight to see him, how he'd grown, he was a bit skinny but visibly thriving on all that fresh air lifestyle he had with his dad. Only seeing them occasionally meant a lot of changes had taken place in their lives too, but this time, they also seemed a lot lighter and no small wonder, how stressed and anxious they must have been at the early stages of my illness, but now we were almost ready for home. All that was left was to have the T. Tube removed and this would mean admittance to the Q.E. overnight.

We had spent almost a week together and it was strange for me to have both the boys with me. I took them on all the local haunts and shared all the things I thought they would be interested in. Having food out at the Inn was good fun for all of us, especially Jonathan's Death by Chocolate experience. He loved chocolate puddings so it was no surprise when he chose this dessert, but something funny was said that caused him to laugh with a mouthful of chocolate pudding and the sight of him laughing set us all off laughing too, and the more he laughed the more we laughed, an unforgettable moment which we still recall whenever Death by Chocolate is chosen. James loved the fishing sprees and I had kept the fishing nets from the Taylors' visit so they came in handy.

I was hoping and praying that the removal of the tube would be as straightforward as the doctors said it should be, because it could have complications like some of the bile escaping into the abdomen causing sharp shoulder pains. Had this happened, it wouldn't have been serious but I was fortunate in that it didn't often occur. I prepared myself and was pretty confident everything would be OK The procedure would not require anaesthetic, it just needed to be pulled out.

Not long after it was removed, I began to have pretty severe pains which were so sore that I felt I would be sick. I was so disappointed and felt like crying but scared, too, that if I began, I would never stop. I kept controlled and tensed up inside which made it worse I suppose, because the pain continued on and on and I had to stay in overnight. I had so much wanted this part to go OK, mostly for the boys' sake, but again there was nothing I could do and I was so fed up.

Eventually I started to pray and ask God if He had a reason for this happening. I started putting into practice the art of accepting what was going on instead and then I started to feel better inside. It was a struggle getting comfy because of the pain, but I slept well and in the morning it was much better and I wandered around the ward and went into the sitting room where I got into a conversation with an Irish woman whose husband had had a liver transplant and was having some complications. Apparently he had been very ill before he had his transplant and had suffered with setbacks. I can't quite remember the nature of his visit to hospital but it soon became apparent that this couple were Christians and were employed in Christian work in Northern Ireland. We talked and shared our common faith and experiences and it was clear that this seemingly chance meeting was another divine appointment. If I hadn't had my complication I would never have met this couple and so never have had the opportunity to share prayers together that morning for John's complete healing. The timing of the Lord is always perfect and so good the way He can work in situations to make His will known. I knew deep down in my heart that, for whatever reason, this couple were needing encouragement just as I had done so many times myself and the Lord proved Himself faithful. We kept in touch with this couple and had the chance to meet them briefly on a visit to Ireland some years later.

Now my family arrived and I was free to go. I waited in the reception until Ivan and the boys drove the car round to the door because it was a bit far for me to walk. Parking at the hospital was a nightmare and it was impossible to find a place anywhere near the entrance. I suppose the sheer volume of staff and visitors arriving there every day was unbelievable and constantly we would hear the sound of car alarms going off. It got to be so common that no one bothered to pay much attention to it after a while, everyone seemed to be oblivious to the noise they made, I must admit I got a bit like that myself. Ivan seemed to be taking a long time in coming round with the car and then he walked in to tell me that the car had gone .... completely gone. It took him by surprise and he even began to wonder if he had just forgotten where he had left it but they all agreed it was definitely gone.

This posed a new problem. Ivan was planning to go north by car catching a sheep sale in Lanark but this had complicated matters, Jonathan and I were flying back together but we needed the car to get to the airport, what on earth could we do? We had to go back to Fiona and Rob's. We had a contact in Birmingham from the Riverside Christian Fellowship, Maggie Bywater. We phoned her for help and she soon sorted things out for us. She took us back to Wolverhampton and we said our farewells to her.

We reported the car missing and the police gave us very little hope of it ever being found. Apparently joy riding was a fashionable pastime for idle young boys in the city and one of their favourite sports to find the waiting cars were hospital car parks. They could be fairly sure that any car parked in a long stay hospital car park was a safe target. We felt it wasn't fair after all that we had been through, we felt we needed things to change for the better and this was just too much.

However, we had things to do before we went and we were going no matter what. We wanted to take Rob and Fiona out for a meal at the Inn up the road and we wanted to repay them in some way for all their kindness and generosity. I found a very suitable card to give them which simply said ....Thank you ....You cared .... You took the time .... You didn't have to.

No, they didn't have to, but they did. I don't remember us discussing it and as I look back it was an imposition to say the least, but I felt so helpless and out of control and for me Fiona's invitation in the hospital that April afternoon was like an invitation from heaven itself. We were desperate and Fiona just came along at the right time. She had no idea what she had let herself in for and if she regretted it I never knew it or felt it. I get completely overwhelmed at their kindness to me, even after all these years have passed, and I will be eternally indebted to them. We gave them a small token gift but really it was just a small thank you. Tell me, how do you go about thanking people for such indescribable self sacrifice? Our gratitude cannot be put into words or money. Their home was indeed like the Bible story where the Shunnamite woman made a little upper room in the wall for the man of God to stay whenever he passed that way and because of her kindness God gave her a son through a prophetic word that Elisha spoke over her. The Lord always blesses kindness shown to strangers. We know and believe God has a wonderful blessing in store for this lovely couple.

It was a very emotional time saying goodbye, they had shared so many of these traumatic moments with us and now here we were at the end of this chapter. Fiona stood on the doorstep with Jonathan and James on either side of her, I took a photo to remind me of the day we left. Many mixed feelings sweeping through my mind, how would I manage on the next phase of my recovery, only time would tell but I felt ready for home now and I wanted to be there more than anything. Inside there was still a lingering fear of being so far away from the hospital where I had become so dependant for so long.

ON CLOUD NINE

Jonathan was my navigator/escort for the next part of the journey, the first leg being by train from Wolverhampton to Birmingham New Street to the airport Birmingham International. We thought we had left plenty of time to make all the right connections but it soon became obvious when we reached Birmingham that we were going to be pushing it to get to the airport on time. It goes without saying that I wasn't very quick over the ground and I hadn't done any running for nearly a year so I was really unfit for what lay ahead. Jonathan was very good and knew where he was going but I found it so hard keeping up with him, firstly checking in here and there, standing in queues and then tearing along to the departure terminal. At least we had a trolley to take the bags. It was all I could do to keep up and gradually I began to panic and thought we were not going to get there on time. I tried to explain at the desk that I was unfit but there were no special arrangements made for invalids. Eventually arriving at the appropriate gate hot and bothered, we still had to walk through a huge long corridor which led straight on to the plane.

Finally, seated in the plane, the tension over, I felt myself going weak at the knees. This was about as much stress as I could handle right now. It took a while for me to calm down but the plane was late in leaving. Jonathan, being young and with bags of confidence, always thought we would make it and so there was no panic in his head. He was more concerned with the thought of getting food served soon, and was rather excited about flying in such a big plane. I must admit I had never been in one so big myself and thankfully by now my original fear of flying had completely gone and I was looking forward to the flight myself.

The whole experience had been so different from my arrival at Birmingham Airport in March when I came down via ambulance flight and got picked up from the plane by a waiting ambulance and then taken directly to the Q.E. It's such an amazing way to travel, rising up over the city and looking down; it seemed incredible that we would be landing in Orkney that same day. The food was delicious and Jonathan soon devoured whatever I wasn't able to eat. The flight was relaxing and trouble free and Aberdeen was our only stop before Orkney.

It was one of those times when I could hardly take in that this was really happening to me. I was really going to be home in a few hours. I tried to keep focused on where we were at now but great excitement was growing in my heart as I contemplated home, my own house, my own sofa, the sheer luxury of my own bed, the view from the kitchen window looking out to the west and the setting sun. How I had missed all that; maybe I didn't now realise just how much.

No long hold ups, we boarded the plane for Orkney. I sensed that Jonathan was rather proud to be escorting me back for the first time, and I was equally proud to be with him. Although so young, he had a maturity beyond his years which gave an unusual sense of stability and assurance. Then again, circumstances had demanded that my family grew up suddenly and I hoped and prayed that it would not damage their future but instead prepare them for the many sudden changes they will no doubt encounter in their own lives. We would all love to cocoon our children and protect them from the worries and cares of life but sometimes it removes the reality of facing things and working them through together. Somehow, I could see this had strengthened my family and made them more appreciative of the value of life, and the fragility of it, too. They no doubt have many of their own peedie thowts, some of which will be too painful to mention yet, but perhaps one day with the passing of time, they will be able to. Time is a great healer.

Being up in the sky naturally gives a totally different dimension to everything and flying made me consider the view God has over His creation. I thought about His perspective as He considers the human beings He has formed, as we scurry around, rushing through our lives. I wondered what He thought of Orkney considering He made it and its inhabitants. I wondered how many of them give a thought for Him or marvel at His handiwork.

I will never forget the feeling I had as I looked down over Orkney for the first time in months. My association with this place was so deep that my whole being was overcome with feelings of ....this is my home............this is where I belong ....how I love this place ....it looks even better than I remember.........flying in over South Ronaldsay and looking out towards Hoy over Orphir and

Stenness ....all the little islands. The coastline, the blue of the sea, the breathtaking colours of the fields with harvest approaching, this remote little place on the face of the earth, so insignificant on a world scale, yet to me it spelt freedom and that sense of being a child again running through the fields at Crook, the wind blowing through my hair, not a care in the world, just me, the wind in the wild and an indescribable inner sense of well being and happiness flooded my soul. Oh it felt so good, so very, very good. These islands of mine were beautiful and now I seemed to see them with new eyes and the feeling of belonging was so deep rooted in me. I hadn't realised how much this place meant to me and I knew that being here would bring healing of the heart.

As we touched down I could hardly believe this was it. I was really home, wonder of wonders, a miracle of modern medicine, a triumph. No wonder I was on cloud nine. Can you get higher than cloud nine? If you can I was there.

HOME SWEET HOME

Home, what a fine word, what a grand feeling, what a marvellous sight as I entered into Howe. The house looked good, spacious and special, it was strange but it looked better, too, than I seemed to have remembered. It was so big compared to Fiona's little city house, every room had so much space and I rejoiced even to see the stairs. I loved the stairs in our house, they were a special feature, even more so with a 'Welcome home Mum' banner. Home was so homely, so welcoming, so cosy and inviting. I took a deep breath and whispered inside, "I'm home. I'm really home."

Sweeter than honey, better than wine,
To be here once again is almost divine.
No words can express, no song ever sung
Can capture the feeling that's just begun
Here in my heart, deep down in my soul
This now has filled that inside hole
Silently missing, empty, alone
Now blissfully satisfied, I'm Home
Sing o my soul, let joy abound
Lift up your voice, praises resound
Life and thanksgiving flowing so free
I'm home, O Jesus, Praise be to Thee.